CUET

(UG) & Integrated PG

2022

Sociology

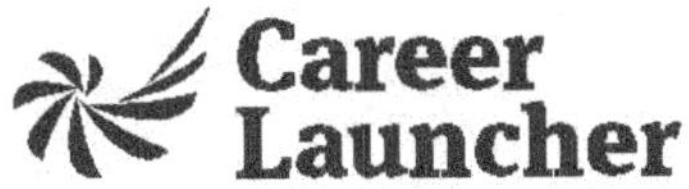

Career
Launcher

Title   : CUET 2022 : Sociology

Language   : English

Editor's Name : Preeti Sagar

Copyright ©   : 2022 CLIP

Typeset & Published by :

Career Launcher Infrastructure (P) Ltd.

A-45, Mohan Cooperative Industrial Area, Near Mohan Estate Metro Station, New Delhi - 110044

Marketed by :

G.K. Publications (P) Ltd.

Plot No. 9A, Sector-27A, Mathura Road, Faridabad, Haryana-121003

ISBN   **: 978-93-95101-23-3**

For product information :
Visit *www.gkpublications.com* or email to *gkp@gkpublications.com*

CONTENTS

About CUET

A year ago, it would have been unimaginable that cut-offs in Delhi University would skyrocket to 100% for some of the undergraduate courses! While DU has always been known for its high cut-offs, there are several other universities where the story is no different.

However, the National Education Policy 2020 (NEP) aims to do away with the tyranny of the ever-rising cut-offs by introducing a Common Entrance Test for all the Central Universities in the country. NEP not only proposes a holistic approach in evaluating the students by giving them the option to select subjects based on their interest, but it also aims to simplify the process of admission to higher-education institutes.

To start with, there would be a Common Entrance Test for all the Central Universities, which would be conducted twice a year from 2022. While this might sound like a new concept to many, the fact is, there is already a CUET, which is conducted for the Central Universities established in or after 2009. As many as 14 of them already admit students based on their performance in the entrance test. The CUET scores are also accepted by four state universities of the country.

The proposed CUET aims to assess conceptual understanding and application of knowledge; and also, to lessen the burden of appearing in multiple tests.

CUET Eligibility

Getting into a premier University is every student's dream. The brand value of the University not only facilitates securing a seat in a master's program in a national/international institute, but also helps in getting job offers through campus placements.

Entry to a Central University, in most cases earlier, was based on merit, i.e., marks secured in Class XII Board exams. However, from the academic year 2021, all Central Universities will also consider the CUET score for admissions into their Undergraduate programs.

CUET 2022: Eligibility Criteria

While the official criteria will be learnt once the CUET 2021 notification is released, the stipulations are not expected to change much from those of previous years.

- A candidate must have passed Class XII (10+2) or equivalent from a recognized education Board.
- If the respective Board awards grades (or CGPA), the conversion factor given by the Board must be used to compute the percentage of marks.
- Candidates, who have completed their Class XII in 2021, and have passed the Board exams, will also be eligible to apply for CUET 2022.

Eligibility: Class XII Students

While CUET is for students who have passed the Class XII (or equivalent) Board exams, any student who is appearing for the Class XII Board exam in 2022 is also eligible to apply for CUET 2021. The candidate would be required to produce the marksheets and relevant certificates as mandated by the participating Central University, and follow the timelines provided for admissions.

Key Points

- Each participating Central University is free to decide its own eligibility criteria for admissions.

- The weightages for CUET and Class XII Board exam results(if, applicable) will be at the sole discretion of the Central University, to which admission is being sought.

- As of date, CUET does not have an age limit. However, Central Universities can fix minimum & maximum age limit for admissions to all (or any) of the programs on offer.

Reservation of Seats

As CUET is an entrance exam for admissions to Undergraduate courses at the Central Universities, which have been established under an Act of the Parliament, each Central University must follow the norms set by the Government of India, with respect to intake and reservation of seats.

Generally, the following break-up is followed:

Category	Reservation
Scheduled Castes	15%
Scheduled Tribes	7.5%
Other Backward Classes (Non-Creamy)	27%
Persons with Disability	5%

Some institutions might even have provisions for the Economically Weaker Sections, which can account for 10% of the total seats. These EWS seats are carved out from the Open Category.

To avail of the reservation benefit based on caste (or any other category as specified), a candidate must be able to produce valid documents/certificates to support such claims.

Conclusion

It is essential for every candidate to check the validity of their candidature for CUET, as well as the Central University he/she is applying to. The candidate should be aware of the documents that might be required while applying for the exam, or during the admissions.

CUET 2022 notification is expected in March 2022, and registration is also going to start then.

CUET: Exam Pattern

Examination Structure for CUET (UG) -2022:

CUET (UG) –2022 will consist of the following 4 Sections:

    Section IA –13 Languages

    Section IB –19 Languages

    Section II –27 Domain specific Subjects

    Section III –General Test

Choosing options from each Section is not mandatory. Choices should match the requirements of the desired University.

Broad features of CUET (UG) -2022 are as follows:

Section	Subjects/ Tests	Questions to be Attempted	Question Type	Duration
Section IA – Languages	There are 13* different languages. Any of these languages may be chosen.	40 questions to be attempted out of 50 in each language	Language to be tested through Reading Comprehension (based on different types of passages–Factual, Literary and Narrative, [Literary Aptitude and Vocabulary]	45 Minutes for each language
Section IB – Languages	There are 19** Languages. Any other language apart from those offered in Section I A may be chosen.			
Section II - Domain	There are 27*** Domains specific subjects being offered under this Section. A candidate may choose a maximum of Six (06) Domains as desired by the applicable University/Universities.	40 Questions to be attempted out of 50	• Input text can be used for MCQ Based Questions • MCQs based on NCERT Class XII syllabus only	
Section III- General Test	For any such undergraduate programme/ programmes being offered by Universities where a General Test is being used for admission.	60 Questions to be attempted out of 75	• Input text can be used for MCQ Based Questions • General Knowledge, Current Affairs, General Mental Ability, Numerical Ability, Quantitative Reasoning (Simple application of basic mathematical concepts arithmetic/algebra geometry/mensuration/s tat taught till Grade 8), Logical and Analytical Reasoning	

* **Languages (13):** Tamil, Telugu, Kannada, Malayalam, Marathi, Gujarati, Odiya, Bengali, Assamese, Punjabi, English, Hindi and Urdu

** **Languages (19):** *French, Spanish, German, Nepali, Persian, Italian, Arabic, Sindhi, Kashmiri, Konkani, Bodo, Dogri, Maithili, Manipuri, Santhali, Tibetan, Japanese, Russian, Chinese.*

*** **Domain Specific Subjects (27):** 1. Accountancy/ Book Keeping 2. Biology/ Biological Studies/ Biotechnology/Biochemistry 3. Business Studies 4. Chemistry 5. Computer Science/ Informatics Practices 6. Economics/ Business Economics 7. Engineering Graphics 8.Entrepreneurship 9. Geography/Geology 10. History 11. Home Science 12.Knowledge Tradition and Practices of India 13. Legal Studies 14. Environmental Science 15. Mathematics 16. Physical Education/ NCC /Yoga 17.Physics 18.Political Science 19. Psychology 20. Sociology 21. Teaching Aptitude 22. Agriculture 23. Mass Media/ Mass Communication 24. Anthropology 25. Fine Arts/Visual Arts (Sculpture/ Painting)/Commercial Arts, 26. Performing Arts – (i) Dance (Kathak/ Bharatnatyam/Oddisi/ Kathakali/Kuchipudi/ Manipuri (ii) Drama- Theatre (iii) Music General (Hindustani/ Carnatic/ RabindraSangeet/ Percussion/ Non-Percussion), 27. Sanskrit *[For all Shastri (Shastri 3 years/ 4 years Honours) Equivalent to B.A./B.A. Honours courses i.e. Shastri in Veda, Paurohitya (Karmakand), Dharamshastra, Prachin Vyakarana, Navya Vyakarana, Phalit Jyotish, Siddhant Jyotish, Vastushastra, Sahitya,Puranetihas, Prakrit Bhasha,Prachin Nyaya Vaisheshik, Sankhya Yoga, Jain Darshan, Mimansa, AdvaitaVedanta, Vishihstadvaita Vedanta, Sarva Darshan, a candidate may choose Sanskrit as the Domain].*

- A Candidate can choose a maximum of **any 3 languages** from Section IA and Section IB taken together. (One of the languages chosen needs to be in lieu of Domain specific subjects)
- Section II offers 27 Subjects, out of which a candidate may choose a **maximum of 6 Subjects.**
- Section III comprises **General Test.**
- For choosing Languages (upto 3) from Section IA and IB and a maximum of 6 Subjects from Section II and General Test under Section III, the Candidate must refer to the requirements of his/her intended University.

Mode of the Test	Computer Based Test-CBT
Test Pattern	Objective type with Multiple Choice Questions
Medium	13 languages (*Tamil, Telugu, Kannada, Malayalam, Marathi, Gujarati, Odiya, Bengali, Assamese, Punjabi, English, Hindi and Urdu*)
Syllabus	**Section IA & IB:** Language to be tested through Reading Comprehension (based on different types of passages–Factual, Literary and Narrative [Literary Aptitude & Vocabulary]
	Section II : As per NCERT model syllabus as applicable to Class XII only
	Section III : General Knowledge, Current Affairs, General Mental Ability, Numerical Ability, Quantitative Reasoning (Simple application of basic mathematical concepts arithmetic/algebra geometry/mensuration/stat taught till Grade 8), Logical and Analytical Reasoning

Level of questions for CUET (UG) -2022:

All questions in various testing areas will be benchmarked at the level of Class XII only. Students having studied Class XII Board syllabus would be able to do well in CUET (UG) – 2022.

Number of attempts:

If any University permits students of previous years of class XII to take admission in the current year also, such students would also be eligible to appear in CUET (UG) – 2022.

Choice of Languages and Subjects:

Generally the languages/subjects chosen should be the ones that a student has opted in his latest Class XII Board examination. However, if any University permits any flexibility in this regards, the same can be exercised under CUET (UG) -2022 also. Candidates must carefully refer to the eligibility requirements of various Central Universities in this regard. Moreover, if the subject to be studied in the Undergraduate course is not available in the list of **27 Domain Specific Subject** being offered, the Candidate may choose the Subject closest to his choice for e.g. For Biochemistry the candidate may choose Biology.

Candidates are advised to visit the NTA CUET (UG)-2022 official website **https://cuet.samarth.ac.in/** for latest updates regarding the Examination.

CUET Syllabus

CUET Syllabus

Before you start your preparation for any entrance exam, it is important to understand the syllabus. Otherwise, your prep will be directionless, and you might be left wondering where things might have gone wrong!

With more than 1.68 lakh seats on offer for the undergraduate courses at the 54 Central Universities, CUET is one the most competitive examinations. For this very reason, while preparing for the exam, you will need to adopt a structured approach. And in doing that, understanding the syllabus is a critical step.

CUET 2022 Overview

CUET 2022 will be a Computer-Based Test (CBT), commonly referred to as an online exam. However, there is a difference between the two terms: CBT and online. In CBT, the questions are kept constant and simply presented in an online format; whereas in an Online Test, questions are stored as a bank, and the system decides which questions are to be presented to the candidate, based on a pre-defined logic.

CUET 2022 is likely to be a General Ability Test, with focus on English Language, Numerical Ability, Logical & Analytical Reasoning, along with General Awareness and Current Affairs.

CUET 2022 Syllabus

The CUET 2022 exam pattern gives a good idea about what is in store for the candidate and how one needs to prepare for the exam.

- **English Language:** The questions in this section will test one's proficiency in the language, based on comprehension passages, fundamentals of grammar, and vocabulary. In the Comprehension section, candidates will be evaluated on their understanding of a passage and its central theme, meanings of words used therein, etc. The Grammar section entails correcting grammatically incorrect sentences, filling of blanks in sentences with appropriate words, etc. Questions on synonyms & antonyms will check one's command over English vocabulary.
- **Numerical Ability:** Questions on Numerical Ability will test the candidate's knowledge of elementary mathematics. Areas like arithmetic, number system, basics of algebra, and modern maths will be central to these types of questions.
- **Logical & Analytical Reasoning:** This section tests the candidate's ability to identify patterns & logical links, and rectify illogical arguments. It can include a variety of Logical Reasoning questions, such as those on syllogisms, logical sequences, analogies, etc., along with Analytical Reasoning questions on series, directions, clocks & calendars, arrangements, and puzzles to name a few.
- **General Awareness and Current Affairs:** The General Awareness section includes static general knowledge, while questions on Current Affairs will gauge a candidate's knowledge of national & international current affairs.

CUET 2022 may or may not have a section on subject knowledge. Once the exam notification is out in March, there will be more clarity on this matter.

While there is no syllabus explicitly mentioned by CUET, the broad idea is always presented. One must look at the previous years' papers and solve the sample papers available to form a basic understanding.

About University of Delhi

University of Delhi (commonly known as DU) was established in 1922 and is one of the largest Universities in the country. With 16 faculties, 86 academic departments, 90 colleges and 540 programs on offer, Delhi University is no doubt one of the sought-after University in the country.

With 1, 96,000 students enrolled in UG programs, Delhi University is a valued university and constantly ranked among the top in the country. DU bagged 11th Rank in NIRF 2020 and ranked 6th in QS India Rankings 2020. The University has two Campuses: North and South.

DU UG Programs

Delhi University offers several programs at the undergraduate level. With more than 60 constituent colleges, the Delhi University offers many undergraduate courses.

Please refer to the table below for the important undergraduate courses offered by the DU and the intake across each program.

Program	Intake
B. A (Pass)	11249
B. A (Hons) Geography	788
B. A (Hons) Economics	2754
B. A (Hons) History	2791
B. A (Hons) Political Science	3657
B. A (Hons) Sociology	596
B. A (Hons) Psychology	670
B. A (Hons) Applied Psychology	252
B. A (Hons) Social Work	133
B. A (Hons) Philosophy	783
B. A (Hons) English	2886
B. A (Hons) Hindi	2829
B. A (Hons) Sanskrit	1407
B. A (Hons) Punjabi	214
B. A (Hons) Urdu	207
BA(Hons) French	49

Program	Intake
BA(Hons) German	49
BA(Hons) Spanish	49
BA(Hons) Italian	49
B. Com (Hons)	7953
B.Com (Pass)	7854
Program	Intake
B.Sc. (H) Biomedical Science	162
B.Sc. (H) Botany	937
B.Sc. (H) Chemistry	1487
B.Sc. (H) Computer Science	1265
B.Sc. (H) Electronics	624
B.Sc. (H) Mathematics	2428
B.Sc. (H) Physics	1659
B.Sc. (H) Zoology	944
B.Sc. Life Sciences	1515
B.Sc. Physical Science with Chemistry	703
B.Sc. Physical Science with Computer Science	553
B.Sc. Physical Science with Electronics	247
B. Sc (Hons.) Statistics	476
B. Sc. (Prog.) Applied Physical Science Industrial Chemistry	96
B.Sc. (Hons.) Home Science	900
B. Sc. (Hons.) Psychology	57
B.Sc. (H) Food Technology	179
B.Sc. (H)Instrumentation	99
B.Sc. (H) Microbiology	238
B.Sc. (H) Polymer Science	59
B.SC. Mathematical Science	224
B.SC. (Hons.) Biochemistry	146
B.SC. Industrial Chemistry	78
B.Sc. (Prog.) Physical Science	940
B.SC. (Hons.) Geology	98

DU UG Programs Eligibility:

As the University offers multiple programs and separate intake for male and female candidates, it is important to check the university official website regularly to keep oneself updated about the eligibility for each program, which can change.

DU UG Admissions:

Until 2021, Delhi University admitted students on the basis of class XII marks. From the academic year 2022, admissions to UG programs offered Delhi University will be based on CUET. CUET will be a common entrance for admissions to UG programs offered by all the Central Universities in the country.

Delhi University UG Programs Reservation:

DU being a Central University offers reservations in admissions according to central government rules.

Schedule Caste (SC): 15% of the total seats are reserved for students who belong to SC category.

Schedule Tribe (ST): 7.5% of the total seats are reserved for students belonging to ST Category.

Other Backward Classes (OBC): 27% of the total intake is reserved for students from Other Backward Classes (OBC), excluding those from creamy layer.

Economically Weaker Section (EWS): The University has reserved 10% seats for EWS category, in accordance with the directive of Ministry of Education.

Persons with Disability (PWD): 5% of the seats are reserved on horizontal basis for students from PWD category.

About BHU

Banaras Hindu University (BHU), situated in the holy city of Varanasi, was founded by Pandit Madan Mohan Malviya in cooperation with Dr. Annie Besant, in 1916 under the act of Parliament-B.H.U Act, 1915. BHU, which is a Central University, comprises of 6 Institutes, 14 Faculties, 144 academic departments, and 4 Inter-disciplinary centers, spread over 1300 acres. The University consists of 15,000 students, 1700 teachers and 8000 non-teaching staff.

BHU was ranked 3rd among the Universities in India in 2020. According to university submissions for NIRF 2021, BHU has 10, 585 students pursuing UG programs, of which 236 students are foreign nationals.

BHU UG Programs

BHU offers a host of undergraduate programs including medical and engineering. Through its various faculties, BHU offers a range of programs which caters to students learning abilities. The University along with its main campus, also offers the undergraduate courses from the following colleges: Mahila Mahavidyalaya (MMV); Arya Mahila Post Graduate College (AMPGC), Vasant Kanya Mahavidyalaya (VKM); Vasanta College for Women (VCW); DAV Post Graduate College (DAVPGC) and Rajiv Gandhi South Campus (RGSC).

Please refer to the table below for the important undergraduate courses offered by BHU and the intake across each program/campuses.

Faculty of Arts				
Course	Campus	Intake	Status	Duration
B.A (Hons) Arts	Faculty of Arts	765	Co-Ed	3 Years
	Mahila Mahavidyalaya	286	Women	3 Years
	Arya Mahila Post Graduate College	383	Women	3 Years
	Vasant Kanya Mahavidyalaya	286	Women	3 Years
	Vasanta College for Women	412	Women	3 Years
	DAV Post Graduate College	309	Co-Ed	3 Years
Faculty of Social Sciences				
Course	Campus	Intake	Status	Duration
B.A (Hons) Social Sciences [incl. B. A (Hons) Economics]	Faculty of Social Sciences	573	Co-Ed	3 Years
	Mahila Mahavidyalaya	193	Women	3 Years
	Arya Mahila Post Graduate College	383	Women	3 Years
	Vasant Kanya Mahavidyalaya	249	Women	3 Years
	Vasanta College for Women	210	Women	3 Years
	DAV Post Graduate College	326	Co-Ed	3 Years

Faculty of Commerce				
Course	Campus	Intake	Status	Duration
B. Com (Hons)	Faculty of Commerce	286	Co-Ed	3 Years
	Vasant Kanya Mahavidyalaya	96	Women	3 Years
	Arya Mahila Post Graduate College	96	Women	3 Years
	DAV Post Graduate College	227	Co-Ed	3 Years
	Rajiv Gandhi South Campus, Mirzapur	114	Co-Ed	3 Years
B. Com (Hons) Financial Markets Management	Faculty of Commerce	62	Co-Ed	3 Years
	Rajiv Gandhi South Campus, Mirzapur	62	Co-Ed	3 Years

Institute of Science				
Course	Campus	Intake	Status	Duration
B.Sc (Hons) Maths Group	Faculty of Science	573	Co-Ed	3 Years
	Mahila Mahavidyalaya	96	Women	3 Years
B.Sc (Hons) Bio Group	Faculty of Science	383	Co-Ed	3 Years
	Mahila Mahavidyalaya	193	Women	3 Years

Faculty of Visual Arts				
Course	Campus	Intake	Status	Duration
B.F.A (Bachelor of Fine Arts)	Faculty of Visual Arts	96	Co-Ed	4 Years
Faculty of Arts				
Bachelor of Vocation (Retail and Logistics Management)	Rajiv Gandhi South Campus	62	Co-Ed	3 Years
Bachelor of Vocation (Hospitality & Tourism Management)	Rajiv Gandhi South Campus	62	Co-Ed	3 Years
Bachelor of Vocation (Fashion Designing and Event Management)	Rajiv Gandhi South Campus	62	Co-Ed	3 Years
Bachelor of Vocation (Modern Office Management)	Rajiv Gandhi South Campus	62	Co-Ed	3 Years
Bachelor of Vocation (Food Processing & Management)	Rajiv Gandhi South Campus	62	Co-Ed	3 Years
Bachelor of Vocation (Medical Lab. & Technology)	Rajiv Gandhi South Campus	62	Co-Ed	3 Years

BHU UG Programs Eligibility:

Each of the courses have different eligibility for admissions. To be eligible for admissions, one must fulfil all the criteria as laid down by the respective faculties of the University.

B.A (Hons) Arts/ B.A (Hons) Social Sciences: Candidate must not be more than 22 years of age and must have passed class XII or equivalent with minimum 50% marks in aggregate.

B.A (Hons) Economics: Candidate must not be more than 22 years of age and must have passed class XII or equivalent with minimum 50% marks in aggregate along with mathematics as one of the papers.

B. Com (Hons)/B. Com (Hons) Financial Markets Management: Candidate must not be more than 22 years of age and must have passed class XII or equivalent with minimum 50% marks in aggregate with Commerce/ Economics/Maths/Computer Science/Finance/Financial Markets Management as one of the subjects.

B. Sc (Hons) Maths Group: Candidate must not be more than 22 years of age and must have passed class XII or equivalent with minimum 50% marks in aggregate in the subjects Physics, Maths plus any one of the following: Chemistry, Statistics, Geology, Computer Science, Information Technology and Geography and must have passed in each of the concerned three subjects.

B. Sc (Hons) Bio Group: Candidate must not be more than 22 years of age and must have passed class XII or equivalent with minimum 50% marks in aggregate in the subjects Physics, Chemistry plus any one of the following: Biology, Geology and Geography and must have passed in each of the concerned three subjects.

B. F. A (Bachelor of Fine Arts): Candidate must not be more than 22 years of age and must have passed class XII or equivalent with minimum 50% marks in aggregate.

Bachelor of Vocation: Candidate must have passed class XII or equivalent in any stream (Science for Food Processing and Medical Lab Technology) or level 4 NSQF certificate.

BHU UG Admissions:

Until 2021, admissions to BHU UG courses were based on Undergraduate Entrance Test (UET) conducted by the University. From the academic year 2022, admissions to UG programs offered by BHU will be based on CUET, which will replace the UET. CUET will be a common entrance for admissions to UG programs offered by all the Central Universities in the country.

BHU UG Programs Reservation:

BHU being a Central University offers reservations in admissions according to central government rules.

Schedule Caste (SC): 15% of the total seats are reserved for students who belong to SC category.

Schedule Tribe (ST): 7.5% of the total seats are reserved for students belonging to ST Category.

Other Backward Classes (OBC): 27% of the total intake is reserved for students from Other Backward Classes (OBC), excluding those from creamy layer.

Economically Weaker Section (EWS): The University has reserved 10% seats for EWS category, in accordance with the directive of Ministry of Education.

Persons with Disability (PWD): 5% of the seats are reserved on horizontal basis for students from PWD category.

About JNU

Ever wondered which University, the cadets from National Defence Academy (NDA) graduate from? Yes. It is Jawaharlal Nehru University (JNU). JNU started in the year 1969, three years after the act of Parliament in 1966. With several academic centres of JNU declared "Centres of Excellence" by the University Grants Commission, JNU has been ranked No. 1 by National Assessment and Accreditation Council (NAAC). JNU has been ranked No. 2 by National Institutional Ranking Framework (NIRF) 2020 and has been awarded the Best University Award by the President of India in 2017. The European Commission has awarded the Jean Monnet Centre of Excellence for European Union Studies in India (CEEUSI) to Jawaharlal Nehru University in 2018. This is one of the highest international recognition for any European Studies programme.

JNU was the first University to start integrated five-year Master of Arts in Language Courses. JNU actively collaborates with National and International Universities for student and faculty exchange programs.

According to university submissions for NIRF 2020, JNU has 1,048 students pursuing UG programs, of which 46 are foreign nationals.

JNU UG Programs

JNU offers a limited program at the undergraduate level, unlike other universities. The focus at undergraduate has been largely on language courses. In 2018, JNU started two programs in engineering and plans to add a few more specializations in future.

Please refer to the table below for the important undergraduate courses offered by JNU and the intake across each program.

School	Program	Intake	Duration
School of Language, Literature and Cultural Studies	B. A (Hons) Pashto	19	3 Years
	B. A (Hons) Persian	39	3 Years
	B. A (Hons) Arabic	39	3 Years
	B. A (Hons) Japanese	48	3 Years
	B. A (Hons) Korean	39	3 Years
	B. A (Hons) Chinese	44	3 Years
	B. A (Hons) French	48	3 Years
	B. A (Hons) German	48	3 Years
	B. A (Hons) Russian	68	3 Years
	B. A (Hons) Spanish	39	3 Years

School of Sanskrit and Indic Studies	B. Sc - M. Sc Integrated Program in Ayurveda Biology	20	5 Years
School of Engineering	B. Tech in Computer Science and Engineering & MS/M. Tech in Social Sciences/Humanities/Science/Technology	25	5 Years
	B. Tech in Electronics and Communication Engineering & MS/M. Tech in Social Sciences/Humanities/Science/Technology	25	5 Years

JNU UG Programs Eligibility:

Each of the courses have different eligibility for admissions. To be eligible for admissions, one must fulfil all the criteria as laid down by the respective faculties of the University.

B.A (Hons) Language Courses: Candidate must not be less than 17 years of age and must have passed Senior School Certificate (10+2) or equivalent examination with minimum of 45% marks.

B. Sc - M. Sc Integrated Program in Ayurveda Biology: Candidate must not be less than 17 years of age and must have passed Senior School Certificate (10+2) or equivalent examination with minimum of 45% marks.

B. Tech-M. Tech: Based on JEE Mains

JNU UG Admissions:

Until 2021, admissions to JNU UG courses were based on JNU Entrance Examination (JNUEE) conducted by the National Testing Agency (NTA). From the academic year 2022, admissions to UG programs offered by JNU will be based on CUET, which will replace the JNUEE. CUET will be a common entrance for admissions to UG programs offered by all the Central Universities in the country.

JNU UG Programs Reservation:

JNU being a Central University offers reservations in admissions according to central government rules.

Schedule Caste (SC): 15% of the total seats are reserved for students who belong to SC category.

Schedule Tribe (ST): 7.5% of the total seats are reserved for students belonging to ST Category.

Other Backward Classes (OBC): 27% of the total intake is reserved for students from Other Backward Classes (OBC), excluding those from creamy layer. Also, Central List of Caste to be followed.

Economically Weaker Section (EWS): The University has reserved 10% seats for EWS category, in accordance with the directive of Ministry of Education.

Persons with Disability (PWD): 5% of the seats are reserved on horizontal basis for students from PWD category.

About Jamia Milia Islamia

Jamia Milia Islamia (JMI) was founded in 1920 in Aligarh and became a Central University in 1988 by the act of Parliament. Jamia in Urdu stands for University and Milia means National, making Jamia Milia Islamia a National University. Jamia Milia Islamia moved to Delhi in 1925 and shifted to its present campus in Okhla in 1935.

Jamia Milia Islamia is a NAAC accredited University with grade "A" and was placed 10th in NIRF Rankings 2020. According to submissions made by University for NIRF 2021, Jamia Milia Islamia has a total of 5,911 students pursuing undergraduate courses at the University, of which 105 are foreign nationals. The University also manage to place a total of 681 UG students with an average salary ranging 4.2 Lacs-6.0 Lacs.

JMI UG Programs

Jamia Milia Islamia (JMI) offers a host of undergraduate programs for students. Through its various faculties, JMI offers a range of programs which caters to students learning abilities.

Please refer to the table below for the important undergraduate courses offered by Jamia Milia Islamia and the intake across each program.

Faculty	Course	Intake	Duration
Faculty of Humanities and Language	B. A (Hons) English	60	3 Years
	B. A (Hons) Hindi	40	3 Years
	B. A (Hons) Mass Media-Hindi	40	3 Years
	B. A (Hons) History	60	3 Years
	Bachelor of Hotel Management (BHM)	40	3 Years
	Bachelor of Tourism and Travel Management	40	3 Years
	B. Voc (Food Production)	40	3 Years
Faculty of Social Sciences	Bachelor of Arts (B. A)	68	3 Years
	B. Com (Hons)	55	3 Years
	BBA (Bachelor of Business Administration)	44	3 Years
	B. A (Hons) Economics	53	3 Years
	B. A (Hons) Sociology	42	3 Years
	B. A (Hons) Political Science	42	3 Years
	B. A (Hons) Psychology	42	3 Years
Faculty of Natural Sciences	B. Sc (Bachelor of Science)	50	3 Years
	B. Sc Biosciences	40	3 Years
	B. Sc Biotechnology	35	3 Years
	B. Sc (Hons) Chemistry	40	3 Years
	B. A/B. Sc (Hons) Geography	60	3 Years
	B. Sc (Hons) Mathematics	45	3 Years
	B. Sc (Hons) Applied Mathematics	45	3 Years
	B. Sc (Hons) Physics	45	3 Years
Faculty of Fine Arts	Bachelor of Fine Arts (Applied Art)	30	4 Years
	Bachelor of Fine Arts (Art Education)	20	4 Years
	Bachelor of Fine Arts (Painting)	20	4 Years
	Bachelor of Fine Arts (Sculpture)	10	4 Years

JMI UG Programs Eligibility:

Each of the courses have different eligibility for admissions. To be eligible for admissions, one must fulfil all the criteria as laid down by the respective faculties of the University.

B. Com (Hons) /BBA /B. A (Hons) Economics: Candidate must have passed class XII or equivalent with a minimum of 50% marks in five subjects.

BHM/BTTM/B. Voc (Food Production): Candidate must have passed class XII or equivalent with a minimum of 45% marks in five subjects.

B. A (Hons) Mass Media/B. A (Hons) Hindi: Candidate must have passed class XII or equivalent with a minimum of 45% marks in five subjects.

B. Sc/B. Sc (Hons): Candidate must have passed class XII or equivalent with minimum 50% marks in each of the science subjects i.e. Physics, Chemistry and Mathematics and 50% marks in aggregate of best 5-subjects.

JMI UG Admissions:

Until 2021, admissions to JMI UG courses were based on Entrance Test (JMI-ET) conducted by the University. From the academic year 2022, admissions to UG programs offered by JMI will be based on CUET, which will replace the JMI-ET. CUET will be a common entrance for admissions to UG programs offered by all the Central Universities in the country.

JMI UG Programs Reservation:

JMI is a minority reservation-based University and accordingly, seats are reserved for candidates as per the norms laid down by the University.

Muslim Minority: 30% of the total seats are reserved for Muslim applicants; 10% of the total seats are reserved for women applicants who are Muslim; 10% of the total intake is for OBC-NC candidates who are Muslims.

Persons with Disability (PWD): 5% of the seats are reserved for students from PWD category.

Jamia Students: 5% seats in all Undergraduate Programs shall be filled by internal students of Jamia who have passed their qualifying examination of the concerned programme (X or XII) from Jamia Schools as regular students.

In addition, Jamia Milia Islamia has supernumerary seats for Kashmiri Migrants and students from Jammu and Kashmir.

About Aligarh Muslim University

Aligarh Muslim University also referred as AMU was established by Sir Syed Ahmad Khan in 1875. The University started as Muhammadan Anglo-Oriental College and became a University (AMU) in 1920. The university has been ranked 801–1000 in the QS World University Rankings of 2021 and 17 in India by the National Institutional Ranking Framework in 2020.

Aligarh Muslim University is institution of national importance, under the seventh schedule of the Constitution of India.

AMU UG Programs

Aligarh Muslim University offers several programs at the undergraduate level. With 7 constituent colleges, the Aligarh Muslim University offers many undergraduate courses.

Please refer to the table below for the important undergraduate courses offered by the AMU and the intake across each program.

Course	Intake	Duration
B. Sc (Hons) Home Science	30*	3 Years
B.Sc (Hons) Agriculture	40	4 Years
B. A (Hons) Arabic	20+10*	3 Years
B. A (Hons) Communicative English	15+20*	3 Years
B. A (Hons) English	40+35*	3 Years
B. A (Hons) Hindi	40+25*	3 Years
B. A (Hons) Geography	50+20*	3 Years
B. A (Hons) Linguistics	20+25*	3 Years
B. A (Hons) Persian	15+25*	3 Years
B. A (Hons) Philosophy	20+10*	3 Years
B. A (Hons) Quaranic Studies	10+10*	3 Years
B. A (Hons) Sanskrit	15+10*	3 Years
B. A (Hons) Urdu	40+50*	3 Years
Bachelor of Fine Arts	15+15*	3 Years
B. Com (Hons)	180+100*	3 Years
B. Voc Production Technology	50	3 Years
B Voc Polymer and Coating Technology	50	3 Years
B. Voc Fashion Design and Garment Technology	50	3 Years
B. A (Hons) Chinese	20	3 Years
B. A (Hons) French	20	3 Years
B. A (Hons) German	20	3 Years

B. A (Hons) Russian	20	3 Years
B. A (Hons) Spanish	20	3 Years
B. Sc (Hons) Biochemistry	30+30*	3 Years
B. Sc (Hons) Botany	60+40*	3 Years
B. Sc (Hons) Zoology	60+45*	3 Years
B. Sc (Hons) Physics	120+35*	3 Years
B. Sc (Hons) Chemistry	120+65*	3 Years
B. Sc (Hons) Mathematics	120+40*	3 Years
B. Sc (Hons) Geography	45+30*	3 Years
B. Sc (Hons) Geology	100+30*	3 Years
B. Sc (Hons) Statistics	60+30*	3 Years
B. Sc (Hons) Industrial Chemistry	20+10*	3 Years
B. Sc (Hons) Computer Applications	40+20*	3 Years

AMU UG Programs Eligibility:

As the University offers multiple programs and separate intake for male and female candidates, it is important to check the university official website regularly to keep oneself updated about the eligibility for each program, which can change.

AMU UG Admissions:

Until 2021, AMU conducted its own entrance test to admit students for the UG programs. From the academic year 2022, admissions to UG programs offered by Aligarh Muslim University will be based on CUET. CUET will be a common entrance for admissions to UG programs offered by all the Central Universities in the country.

University of Allahabad UG Programs Reservation:

Allahabad University being a Central University offers reservations in admissions according to central government rules. Kindly check the university website for further details.

SOCIOLOGY
PART – I

Introducing Indian Society

Problems in Society and Perceptions

The knowledge about society is acquired without explicit teaching as it is such an integral part of the process of growing up, knowledge about society seems to be acquired "naturally" or "automatically". Our social context shapes our opinions, beliefs and expectations about society and social relations. These beliefs are not necessarily wrong, though they can be. The problem is that they are 'partial' which has meaning in two different ways - incomplete (the opposite of whole), and biased (the opposite of impartial). So our 'unlearnt' knowledge or common sense usually allows us to see only a part of social reality. However, sociology does not offer a solution to this problem in the form of a perspective.

What Sociology Provides?

- Understanding Indian society and its structure provides a sort of social map on which you could locate yourself.

- Sociology tells you about what kinds of groups or groupings there are in society, what their relationships are to each other, and what this might mean in terms of your own life.

- C.Wright Mills, a well-known American sociologist has written, sociology can help you to map the links and connections between "personal troubles" and "social issues". By personal troubles Mills means the kinds of individual worries, problems or concerns that everyone has.

Societal Issues

- The "generation gap" or friction between older and younger generations is a social phenomenon which is common to many societies and many time periods.

- Unemployment or the effects of a changing occupational structure is also a societal issue, that concerns millions of different kinds of people. It includes the sudden increase in job prospects for information technology related professions, as well as the declining demand for agricultural labour.

- Issues of communalism or the animosity of one religious community towards another, or casteism, which is the exclusion or oppression of some castes by others, are again society-wide problems.

- Gender inequality, as both male and female being distinct social groups are affected by this but in a different way.

Colonialism and Indian Society

- Indian consciousness took shape during colonial period.

- Colonial rule unified all of India for the first time, and brought in the forces of modernisation and capitalist economic change.

- The economic, political and administrative unification of India under colonial rule was achieved at great expense.

- Colonial exploitation and domination scarred Indian society in many ways.

- Colonialism also gave birth to its own enemy - nationalism. Indian nationalism took shape during British colonialism.

- The shared experience of colonial domination helped unify and energise different sections of the community.

- The emerging middle classes began, with the aid of western style education, to challenge colonialism on its own ground.

- Ironically, colonialism and western education also gave the impetus for the rediscovery of tradition. This led to the developments on the cultural and social front which solidified emergent forms of community at the national and regional levels.

- Colonialism created new classes and communities which came to play significant roles in subsequent history.

- The urban middle classes were the main carriers of nationalism and they led the campaign for freedom.

- Colonial interventions also crystallised religious and caste based communities. These too became major players.

Exercise

1. In the context of sociology, the term reflexivity is -
   - (a) Making perceptions about others
   - (b) Resolving social problems on the basis of evidences
   - (c) Self-inspection about social problems
   - (d) All of the above

2. Which of the following states have smaller area than Arunachal Pradesh?
   - (a) Manipur
   - (b) Telangana
   - (c) Andhra Pradesh
   - (d) Rajasthan

3. What does sociologist believe regarding problems in society?
   - (a) There is a rational view about the society.
   - (b) No ideal vantage point exists.
   - (c) Problems can be solved through common sense.
   - (d) Unlearnt knowledge can be used to solve problems.

4. Sociology can help you to map the links and connections between "personal troubles" and "social issues". Which of the following personality has stated the mentioned statement?
   - (a) Mahatma Gandhi
   - (b) James Mills
   - (c) C. Wright Mills
   - (d) Emanuel Kant

5. In Sociology, the "generation gap" or friction between older and younger generations, is which of the following type of problem?
   - (a) Social issues
   - (b) Personal problem
   - (c) Both (a) and (b)
   - (d) Neither (a) nor (b)

6. Unemployment is which of the following type of issue in Sociology?
   - (a) Economic issue
   - (b) Personal issue
   - (c) Lack of qualification
   - (d) Social issue

7. Which of the following issues lead to unemployment?
   1. Sudden increase in job prospects for information technology related profession
   2. Declining demand for agricultural labour
   3. Lack of skills as per the market

   Select the correct answer using the code given below:
   - (a) 1 and 2 only
   - (b) 2 and 3 only
   - (c) 3 only
   - (d) 1, 2 and 3

8. Which of the following were the results of colonization in India?
   1. Political and economic unification of India
   2. Administrative unification of India
   3. Modernization
   4. Nationalism

   Select the correct answer using the code given below:
   - (a) 1, 2 and 3 only
   - (b) 2, 3 and 4 only
   - (c) 3 and 4 only
   - (d) All of the above

9. Through which of the following ways, Indian nationalism took shape under British colonialism?
   1. Shared experience of colonial domination
   2. Emerging middle classes with the aid of traditional Indian and western education
   3. Rediscovery of Indian tradition

   Select the correct answer using the code given below:
   - (a) 1 and 3 only
   - (b) 2 and 3 only
   - (c) 3 only
   - (d) All of the above

10. Which of the following section of society were the main carriers of nationalism in India?
    - (a) Sepoys
    - (b) Urban middle class
    - (c) Workers
    - (d) Revolutionaries

Answer Keys

1. (c)   **2.** (a)   **3.** (b)   **4.** (c)   **5.** (a)   **6.** (d)   **7.** (d)   **8.** (d)   **9.** (a)   **10.** (b)

The Demographic Structure of Indian Society

Chapter at Glance

- Demography is the systematic study of population has Greek origin and composed of the two words, demos (people) and graphein (describe) which implies the description of people.

- Demography studies the trends and processes associated with population including
  - changes in population size;
  - patterns of births, deaths, and migration;
  - the structure and composition of the population, such as the relative proportions of women, men and different age groups.

- Different varieties of demography -
  - formal demography which is a largely quantitative field
  - social demography focuses on the social, economic or political aspects of populations

- All demographic studies are based on processes of counting or enumeration - census or survey which involves systemic collection of data on the people residing within a specified territory.

- Social statistics - quantitative data on various aspects of the population and economy.

- The American census of 1790 was probably the first modern census, and the practice was soon taken up in Europe as well in the early 1800s.

- In India, censuses began to be conducted by the British Indian government between 1867-72, and regular ten yearly (or decennial) censuses have been conducted since 1881.

- Independent India continued the practice, started in 1951, the most recent being in 2011. The Indian census is the largest such exercise in the world (since China, which has a slightly larger population, does not conduct regular censuses).

Importance of Demographic Data

- Demographic data are important for the planning and implementation of state policies, specially for economic development and general public welfare.

- Aggregate statistics or the numerical characteristics that refer to a large collectivity consisting of millions of people which offer a concrete and strong argument for the existence of social phenomena.

- Formal demography is primarily concerned with the measurement and analysis of the components of population change.

- Its focus is on quantitative analysis for which it has a highly developed mathematical methodology suitable for forecasting population growth and changes in the composition of population.

Theories and Concepts in Demography

Malthusian Theory

- English political economist Thomas Robert Malthus theory of population growth that outlined in his Essay on Population (1798), was a rather pessimistic one.

- He argued that human populations tend to grow at a much faster rate than the rate at which the means of human subsistence (specially food, but also clothing and other agriculture-based products) can grow.

- Humanity is condemned to live in poverty forever because the growth of agricultural production will always be overtaken by population growth.

- While population rises in geometric progression (i.e., like 2, 4, 8, 16, 32 etc.), agricultural production can only grow in arithmetic progression (i.e., like 2, 4, 6, 8, 10 etc.).

- 'Preventive checks' is a way to control population through postponing marriage or practicing sexual abstinence or celibacy.

- Malthus believed therefore that 'positive checks' to population growth - in the form of famines and diseases were inevitable as they were nature's way of dealing with the imbalance between food supply and increasing population.

Theory of Disapproved by Other Theories

- The pattern of population growth began to change in the latter half of nineteenth century, and by the end of the first quarter of the twentieth century these changes were quite dramatic.

- Birth rates had declined, and outbreaks of epidemic diseases were being controlled.

- Malthus's predictions were proved false because both food production and standards of living continued to rise despite the rapid growth of population.

- Malthus was also criticised by liberal and Marxist scholars for asserting that poverty was caused by population growth.

- The critics argued that problems like poverty and starvation were caused by the unequal distribution of economic resources rather than by population growth.

- An unjust social system allowed a wealthy and privileged minority to live in luxury while the vast majority of the people were forced to live in poverty.

Theory of Demographic Transition

- It suggested that population growth is linked to overall levels of economic development and that every society follows a typical pattern of developmentrelated population growth.

- Three basic stages of population growth -

  - The first stage is that of low population growth in a society that is underdeveloped and technologically backward.

  - Second stage - Growth rates are low because both the death rate and the birth rate are very high, so that the difference between the two (or the net growth rate) is low.

  - The third (and last) stage is also one of low growth in a developed society where both death rate and birth rate have been reduced considerably and the difference between them is again small.

  - Between these two stages is a transitional stage of movement from a backward to an advanced stage, and this stage is characterised by very high rates of growth of population.

- 'Population explosion' happens because death rates are brought down relatively quickly through advanced methods of disease control, public health, and better nutrition.

- It takes longer for society to adjust to change and alter its reproductive behaviour (which was evolved during the period of poverty and high death rates) to suit the new situation of relative prosperity and longer life spans.

- In India too, the demographic transition is not yet complete as the mortality rate has been reduced but the birth rate has not been brought down to the same extent.

Some Indicators of Population Growth

- Birth rate is the total number of live births in a particular area (an entire country, a state, a district or other territorial unit) during a specified period (usually a year) divided by the total population of that area in thousands. In other words, the birth rate is the number of live births per 1000 population.

- The death rate is a similar statistic, expressed as the number of deaths in a given area during a given time per 1000 population. These statistics depend on the reporting of births and deaths by the families in which they occur.

- The rate of natural increase or the growth rate of population refers to the difference between the birth rate and the death rate.

  - When difference is 'zero' or less, population is 'stabilized' or has reached the 'replacement level' that is the rate of growth required for new generations to replace the older ones that are dying out.

- Negative growth rate means fertility levels are below the replacement level. Japan, Russia, Italy and Eastern Europe are some examples of it.

- The fertility rate refers to the number of live births per 1000 women in the child-bearing age group, usually taken to be 15 to 49 years. This is a 'crude' rate which is a rough average for an entire population and does not take into account the differences across age-groups.

- Total fertility rate refers to the total number of live births that a hypothetical woman would have if she lived through the reproductive age group and had the average number of babies in each segment of this age group as determined by the age-specific fertility rates for that area.

- The infant mortality rate is the number of deaths of babies before the age of one year per 1000 live births.

- The maternal mortality rate is the number of women who die in childbirth per 1,00,000 live births.

- High rate of infant and maternal mortality rates indicates backwardness and poverty. Improvement in these rates indicates improved medical facilities, level of education, awareness and prosperity.

- The sex ratio refers to the number of females per 1000 males in a given area at a specified time period.
  - Naturally, 943 to 952 female babies for every 1000 males are considered as sext ratio is in favor of females. The reasons are -
    i. Girl babies appear to have an advantage over boy babies in terms of resistance to disease in infancy.
    ii. At the other end of the life cycle, women have tended to outlive men in most societies, so that there are more older women than men.
  - Countries like China, South Korea and India, sex ratio is declining due to 'son preference' and negligence to girl child.
  - the age structure of the population refers to the proportion of persons in different age groups relative to the total population. Factors -
  - poor medical facilities,
  - prevalence of disease
  - other factors like quality of live, development, etc.
  - the dependency ratio is a measure comparing the portion of a population which is composed of dependents (i.e., elderly people who are too old to work, and children who are too young to work) with the portion that is in the working age group, generally defined as 15 to 64 years.

Dependency ratio (%)

$$= \frac{\text{population below 15 or above 64}}{\text{population in the 15-64 age group}}$$

  - rising dependency ratio leads to ageing population i.e. cause for worry
  - falling dependency ratio I source of economic growth and prosperity.
  - demographic dividend - less ageing population and high working population benefits country which flow from the changing age structure. This benefit is temporary because the larger pool of working age people will eventually turn into non-working old people.

Size and Growth of India's Population

- India is the second most populous country in the world after China.
- Before 1931, both death rates and birth rates were high, whereas, after this transitional moment the death rates fell sharply but the birth rate only fell slightly.

- The principal reasons for the decline in the death rate after 1921 were increased levels of control over famines and epidemic diseases.
- The major epidemic diseases in the past were fevers of various sorts, plague, smallpox and cholera.
- Epidemic was controlled by - improvements in medical cures for these diseases, programmes for mass vaccination, and efforts to improve sanitation
- Famines were also a major and recurring source of increased mortality. Famines were caused by high levels of continuing poverty and malnutrition in an agro-climatic environment that was very vulnerable to variations in rainfall.

Factors

- Lack of adequate means of transportation and communication
- Inadequate efforts of states to control the situation
- The Mahatma Gandhi National Rural Employment Guarantee Act is the latest state initiative to tackle the problem of hunger and starvation in rural areas.

Variation in Fertility Rates in India

- Unlike the death rate, the birth rate has not registered a sharp fall as birth rate is a sociocultural phenomenon that is relatively slow to change.
- Increased levels of prosperity exert a strong downward pull on the birth rate.
- Once infant mortality rates decline, and there is an overall increase in the levels of education and awareness, family size begins to fall.
- Some states, like Andhra Pradesh, Himachal Pradesh, Punjab, Tamil Nadu and West Bengal have managed to bring down their total fertility rates (TFR) to 1.7 each (2016). This means that the average woman in these states produces only 1.7 children, which is below the 'replacement level' and Kerala's TFR is also below the replacement level, which means that the population is going to decline in future.
- Bihar, Madhya Pradesh, Rajasthan and Uttar Pradesh, which still have very high TFRs. In 2016, the TFRs of these states were 3.3, 2.8, 2.7 and 3.1, respectively.
- According to the Economic Survey 2018-19, India's total birth rate was 22.4, among them rural birth rate was 22.4 and urban birth rate was 17.3.
- The highest birth rate in India is of Uttar Pradesh (25.9) and Bihar (26.4), and they will also account for about half (50%) of the additions to the Indian population upto the year 2041.

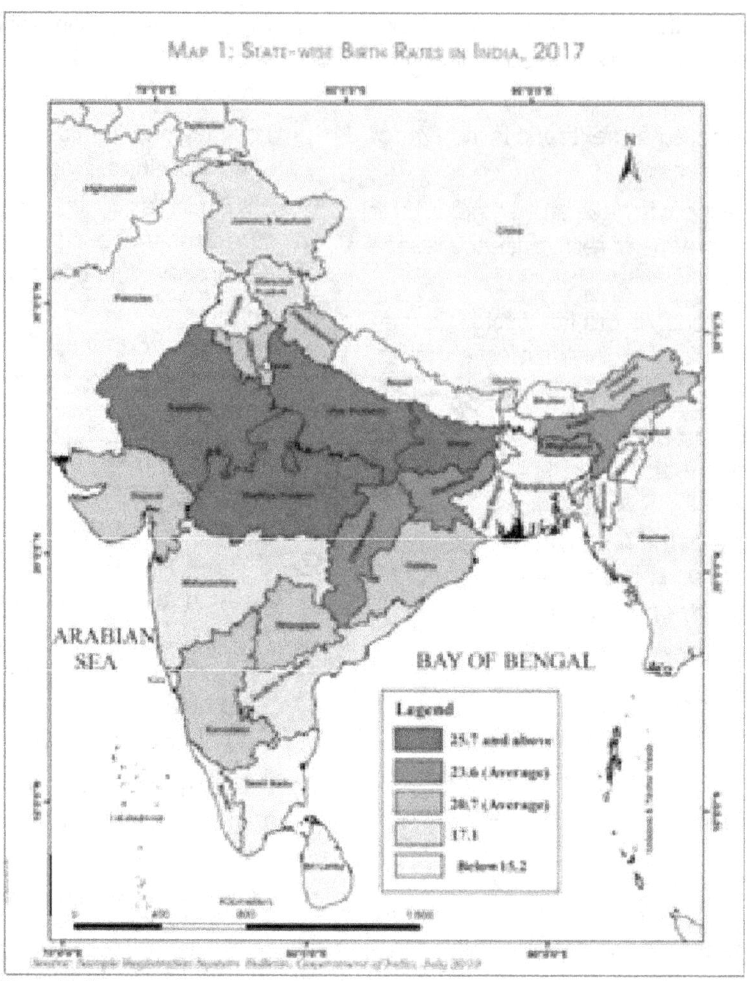

Age Structure of Indian Population

- India has a very young population - that is, the majority of Indians tend to be young, and the average age is also less than that for most other countries.

- The bias towards younger age groups in the age structure is believed to be an advantage for India. Like the East Asian economies in the past decade and like Ireland today, India is supposed to be benefitting from a 'demographic dividend'.

- This dividend arises from the fact that the current generation of working-age people is a relatively large one, and it has only a relatively small preceding generation of old people to support.

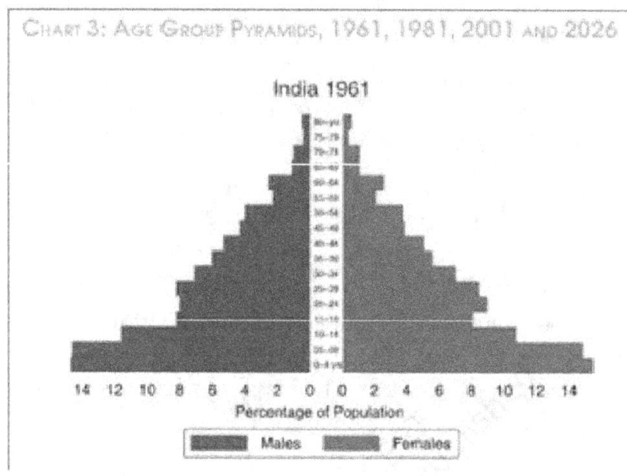

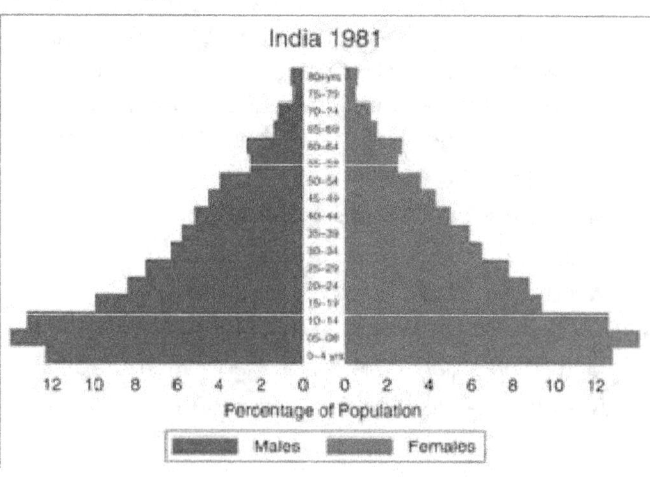

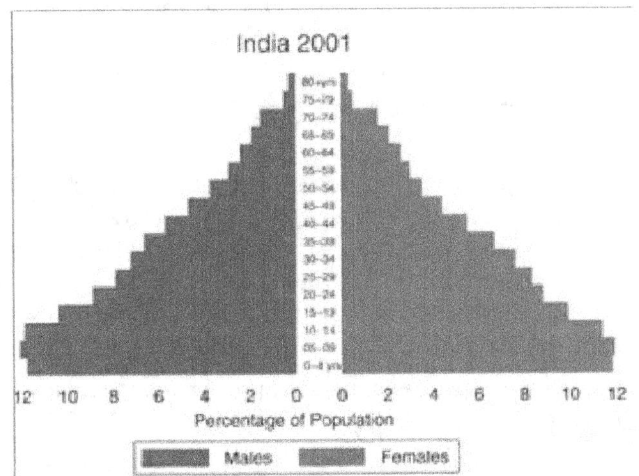

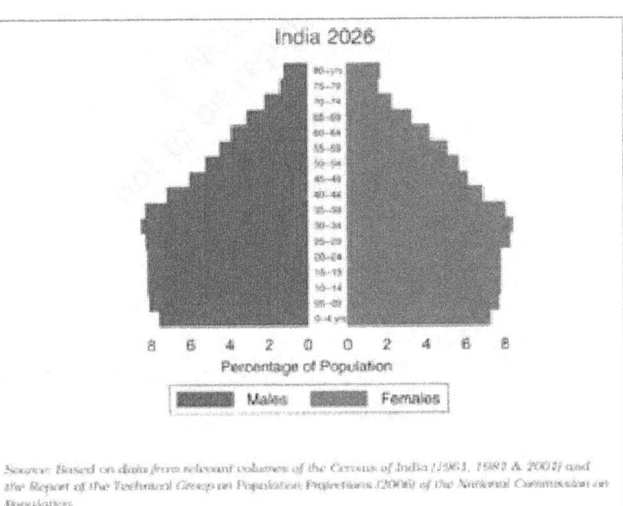

Source: Based on data from relevant volumes of the Census of India (1961, 1981 & 2001) and the Report of the Technical Group on Population Projections (2006) of the National Commission on Population.

- As with fertility rates, there are wide regional variations in the age structure as well. While a state like Kerala is beginning to acquire an age structure like that of the developed countries, Uttar Pradesh presents a very different picture with high proportions in the younger age groups and relatively low proportions among the aged.

- India as a whole is somewhere in the middle, because it includes states like Uttar Pradesh as well as states that are more like Kerala.

Declining Sex Ratio in India

- Historically, the sex ratio has been slightly in favour of females, that is, the number of females per 1000 males has generally been somewhat higher than 1000. However, India has had a declining sex-ratio for more than a century.

- From 972 females per 1000 males at the turn of the twentieth century, the sex ratio has declined to 933 at the turn of the twenty-first century.

- According to Census of India 2011 sex ratio has increased and now it is 943 females per 1000 males.

- Age specific sex ratios began to be computed in 1961.

- As many as nine States and Union Territories have a child sex ratio of under 900 females per 1000 males.

- Haryana is the worst state with an incredibly low child sex ratio of 793 (the only state below 800), followed by Punjab, Jammu & Kashmir, Delhi, Chandigarh, Uttarakhand and Himachal Pradesh.

- Uttar Pradesh, Daman & Diu, Himachal Pradesh, Lakhshadweep and Madya Pradesh are all under 925, while large states such as West Bengal, Assam, Bihar, Tamil Nadu, Andhra Pradesh, Karnataka are above the national average of 919 but below the 970-mark.

- Even Kerala, the state with the better overall sex ratio does not do too well at 964, while the highest child sex ratio of 972 is found in Arunachal Pradesh.

Reasons of Decline

- The health factor that affects women differently from men is childbearing.

- Improvement in maternal mortality rate

- Improved level of nutrition

- General education and awareness

- Improvement in available medical and communication facilities

Factors Leading to Decline

- Severe neglect of girl babies in infancy leads higher death rates

- sex-specific abortions that prevent girl babies from being born

- female infanticide (or the killing of girl babies due to religious or cultural beliefs)

- According to the Economic Survey for a recent year, Maharashtra, Punjab, Haryana, Chandigarh and Delhi are having high per capita income and the child sex ratio of these states is still low. So the problem of selective abortions is not due to poverty or ignorance or lack of resources.

- It is also possible (though this issue is still being researched) that as economically prosperous families decide to have fewer children - often only one or two now - they may also wish to choose the sex of their child.

Policies to Improve Sex Ratio

- Laws banning practice of sex determination and imposing heavy fines and imprisonment as punishment. Known as the Pre-natal Diagnostic

Techniques (Regulation and Prevention of Misuse) Act has been in force since 1996, and has been further strengthened in 2003.

- Recently, the Government of India has introduced the programme, 'Beti-Bachao, BetiPadhao'. It can prove to be an important policy to increase the child sex ratio in the country.

Literacy

- Literacy as a prerequisite to education is an instrument of empowerment

- Literacy levels have improved considerably after independence, and almost two-thirds of our population is now literate.

- But improvements in the literacy rate have to struggle to keep up with the rate of growth of the Indian population, which is still quite high.

- Literacy rates also vary by social group - historically disadvantaged communities like the Scheduled Castes and Scheduled Tribes have lower rates of literacy, and rates of female literacy within these groups are even lower.

- Regional variations are still very wide, with states like Kerala approaching universal literacy, while states like Bihar are lagging far behind.

- The inequalities in the literacy rate are specially important because they tend to reproduce inequality across generations.

Rural-Urban Differences

- According to Census of India 2011 still more people are living in rural areas but the population of urban areas has increased.

- Now 68.8% population lives in rural areas while 31.2% people live in urban areas.

- Agriculture used to be by far the largest contributor to the country, but today it only contributes about one-sixth of the gross domestic product.

- Mass media and communication channels are now bringing images of urban life styles and patterns of consumption into the rural areas.

- Consequently, urban norms and standards are becoming well known even in the remote villages, creating new desires and aspirations for consumption.

Mass transit and mass communication are bridging the gap between the rural and urban areas.

- The rapid growth in urbanisation shows that the town or city has been acting as a magnet for the rural population.

- Those who cannot find work (or sufficient work) in the rural areas go to the city in search of work. This flow of rural-tourban migration has also been accelerated by the continuous decline of common property resources like ponds, forests and grazing lands.

- These common resources enabled poor people to survive in the villages although they owned little or no land.

- For the socially oppressed groups like the Scheduled Castes and Scheduled Tribes, this may offer some partial protection from the daily humiliation they may suffer in the village where everyone knows their caste identity.

- The anonymity of the city also allows the poorer sections of the socially dominant rural groups to engage in low status work that they would not be able to do in the village.

- There are now 5,161 towns and cities in India, where 286 million people live. However, is that more than two-thirds of the urban population lives in 27 big cities with million-plus populations.

Population Policy in India

- India was the first country to explicitly announce a population policy in 1952.

- The population policy took the concrete form of the National Family Planning Programme.

- The broad objectives of this programme have remained the same - to try to influence the rate and pattern of population growth in socially desirable directions.

- The most important objective was to slow down the rate of population growth through the promotion of various birth control methods, improve public health standards, and increase public awareness about population and health issues.

- In 2017, Government of India came out with National Health Policy 2017 in which most of the socio-demographic goals were incorporated with new targets.

Exercise

1. Which of the following factors are not associated with the nation-state?
   - (a) Public health management system
   - (b) Governance
   - (c) Economic policies
   - (d) Authoritarian power

2. 'Essay on population' is a work of which of the following thinker?
   - (a) Thomas Robert Malthus
   - (b) C. Wright Mills
   - (c) Karl Marx
   - (d) None of the above

3. Demography is important because of the following reason -
   - (a) To update total births and deaths in a year
   - (b) To expand sphere of state activity
   - (c) To count increased number of voters
   - (d) To provide governance in the country

4. **Assertion (A):** Indian census gives demographic data which is largest such exercise in the world.

   Reason (R): Demographic data is important for the planning and implementation of state policies.
   - (a) Both A and R are true and R is the correct explanation of A.
   - (b) Both A and R are true and R is not the correct explanation of A.
   - (c) A is true and R is false
   - (d) Both A and R are false

5. Which of the following are preventive checks to control population?
   - (a) Use of contraceptives
   - (b) Enforcement of family planning
   - (c) High number of natural deaths
   - (d) Celibacy and postponing marriages

6. **Assertion (A):** Malthus believes there were positive checks to control population.

   Reason (R): Positive checks inevitable as they were nature's way of dealing with the imbalance between food supply and increasing population.
   - (a) Both A and R are true and R is the correct explanation of A.
   - (b) Both A and R are true and R is not the correct explanation of A.
   - (c) A is true and R is false
   - (d) Both A and R are false

7. **Assertion (A):** Poverty causes by population growth.

   Reason (R): Unequal distribution of economic resources causes poverty and starvation.
   - (a) Both A and R are true and R is the correct explanation of A.
   - (b) Both A and R are true and R is not the correct explanation of A.
   - (c) A is true and R is false
   - (d) Both A and R are false

8. Which of the following is correct representation of theory of demographic transition?
   - (a) Very high birth and death rate - technologically backward society - reduction in birth and death rate
   - (b) Reduction in birth and death rate - technologically backward society - very high birth and death rate
   - (c) Technologically backward society - very high birth and death rate - reduction in birth and death rate
   - (d) Technologically backward society - very high birth and death rate

9. Population explosion takes place due to which of the following reason?
   - (a) Reduction in death rates at slow pace
   - (b) Increase in birth rate quickly
   - (c) Both birth and death rates increases at massive scale
   - (d) Quick reduction in death rates due to improved nutrition

10. The difference between birth rate and death rate refers to -
    - (a) Fertility rate
    - (b) Rate of natural increase of population
    - (c) Total fertility rate
    - (d) Replacement level

11. Replacement level of population in a country represents
    - (a) Stabilized population
    - (b) Economic growth stabilizes
    - (c) Hampers economic growth
    - (d) High death rate among old age population

12. Japan and Eastern Europe are experiencing negative growth due to -
    - (a) High fertility rate
    - (b) Low replacement level
    - (c) Stagnant technological advancement
    - (d) Fertility levels are below the replacement level

13. Which of the following demographic indicator is not considered while calculating fertility rate?

(a) Differences across age-groups

(b) Number of live births per 1000 women in child-bearing age group

(c) Rough average of entire population

(d) Crude rate

14. Which of the following indicator is not correct regarding maternal mortality rate?

(a) High maternal mortality rate indicates backwardness and poverty

(b) Number of women dies in child birth per 1000 live births

(c) Improved medical facilities help to fall down maternal mortality rate

(d) Awareness and prosperity lowers down maternal mortality rate

15. Which of the statements is not correct regarding sex ratio?

(a) China and South Korea is having low sex ratio

(b) Decline in sex ratio in Asia is found due to son preference

(c) There had been slightly more female than male in many countries

(d) All of the above

16. Which of the following factors lead to fall in the family size?

I.   Increased level of education

II. Awareness

III. Decline in infant mortality rates

(a) I and II   (b) II and III

(c) I and III   (d) I, II and III

17. Kerala's TFR is below the replacement level, what does it imply?

(a) Population is not stabilized

(b) Old population is greater in number than the younger ones

(c) Population is going to decline in future

(d) Population will increase

18. Which of the following factors held responsible for declining sex ratio in India?

I.   Neglect of girl child in infancy

II. Sex-specific abortions

III. Female infanticide

(a) I and II

(b) I and III

(c) II and III

(d) I, II and III

19. Assertion (A): The lowest child sex ratios are found in the most prosperous regions of India.

Reason (R): The problem of selective abortions is due to poverty or ignorance or lack of resources.

(a) Both A and R are true and R is the correct explanation of A.

(b) Both A and R are true and R is not the correct explanation of A.

(c) A is true and R is false

(d) Both A and R are false

Read the given image and answer the questions 20, 21 and 22.

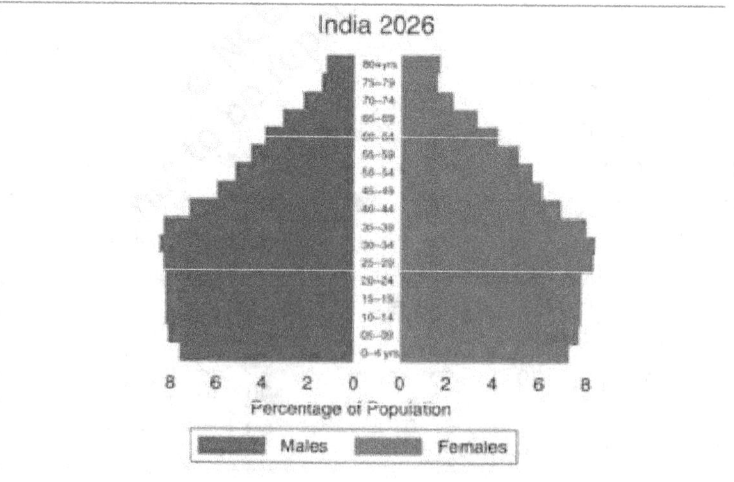

Source: Based on data from relevant volumes of the Census of India (1961, 1981 & 2001) and the Report of the Technical Group on Population Projections (2006) of the National Commission on Population.

20. The middle of given pyramid is wider, what does it imply?

    (a) Increase in total population

    (b) Fall in middle age population

    (c) Birth rate is slow

    (d) Death rate is higher

21. If more and more people began to live, the top of pyramid will grow wider, what does it mean?

    (a) High birth rate

    (b) Low death rate

    (c) Rise in life expectancy

    (d) Demographic transition

22. As shown in the figure, how middle age group population is considerable for the country?

    (a) Better medical facilities

    (b) Better nutrition

    (c) Increase in unemployment

    (d) Demographic dividend

Read the following passage and answer the questions 23, 24 and 25.

The 'demographic dividend' results from an increase in the proportion of workers relative to non-workers in the population. In terms of age, the working population is roughly that between 15 and 64 years of age. This working age group must support itself as well as those outside this age group (i.e., children and elderly people) who are unable to work and are therefore dependents.

Changes in the age structure due to the demographic transition lower the 'dependency ratio', or the ratio of non-working age to working-age population, thus creating the potential for generating growth. But this potential can be converted into actual growth only if the rise in the working age group is accompanied by increasing levels of education and employment.

23. As demographic dividend of India is in favor, but the potential of population need to be converted into actual growth through which of the following ways?

    (a) Improvement in medical facilities

    (b) Education and employment

    (c) Urbanization

    (d) Establishment of more and more industries

24. Which of the following section of population is considered as dependents?

    I. Women

    II. Children below 14 years of age

    III. Elderly people above 64

    (a) I only   (b) II and II

    (c) I and II   (d) All of the above

25. Changes in the age structure due to demographic transition leads to -

    (a) Lower dependency ratio

    (b) Higher dependency ratio

    (c) Demographic dividend

    (d) Stabilizes population

Answer Keys

1. (d)	**2.** (a)	**3.** (b)	**4.** (a)	**5.** (d)	**6.** (a)	**7.** (b)	**8.** (c)	**9.** (d)	**10.** (b)
11. (a)	**12.** (d)	**13.** (a)	**14.** (b)	**15.** (b)	**16.** (d)	**17.** (c)	**18.** (d)	**19.** (c)	**20.** (a)
21. (c)	**22.** (d)	**23.** (b)	**24.** (b)	**25.** (a)					

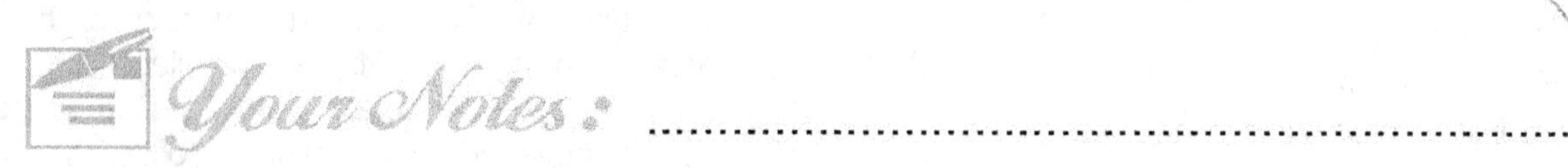

Your Notes :

Social Institutions Continuity and Change

Caste and the Caste System

'Caste' is the name of an ancient social institution that has been part of Indian history and culture for thousands of years.

- Caste is an institution uniquely associated with the Indian sub-continent.
- Although it is an institution characteristic of Hindu society, caste has spread to the major non-Hindu communities of the Indian sub-continent. This is specially true of Muslims, Christians and Sikhs.
- As is well-known, the English word 'caste' is actually a borrowing from the Portuguese casta, meaning pure breed.
- The word refers to a broad institutional arrangement that in Indian languages (beginning with the ancient Sanskrit) is referred to by two distinct terms, varna and jati.
- Varna, literally 'colour', is the name given to a four-fold division of society into brahmana, kshatriya, vaishya and shudra.
- Varna excludes a significant section of the population composed of the 'outcastes', foreigners, slaves, conquered peoples and others, sometimes referred to as the panchamas or fifth category.
- Jati is a generic term referring to species or kinds of anything, ranging from inanimate objects to plants, animals and human beings.
- The four varna classification is common to all of India, the jati hierarchy has more local classifications that vary from region to region.

Caste in the Past

- In its earliest phase, in the late Vedic period roughly between 900 - 500 BC, the caste system was really a varna system and consisted of only four major divisions. These divisions were not very elaborate or very rigid, and they were not determined by birth.

- It is only in the post Vedic period that caste became the rigid institution that is familiar to us from well-known definitions.
- The most commonly cited defining features of caste are the following:
  - Caste is determined by birth - a child is "born into" the caste of its parents. One can never change one's caste, leave it, or choose not to join it, although there are instances where a person may be expelled from their caste.
  - Membership in a caste involves strict rules about marriage. Caste groups are "endogamous", i.e. marriage is restricted to members of the group.
  - Caste membership also involves rules about food and food-sharing. What kinds of food may or may not be eaten is prescribed and who one may share food with is also specified.
  - Caste involves a system consisting of many castes arranged in a hierarchy of rank and status.
  - Castes also involve sub-divisions within themselves, i.e., castes almost always have sub-castes and sometimes sub-castes may also have subsub-castes.
  - Castes were traditionally linked to occupations. A person born into a caste could only practice the occupation associated with that caste, so that occupations were hereditary, i.e. passed on from generation to generation.
- Theoretically, the caste system can be understood as the combination of two sets of principles, one based on difference and separation and the other on wholism and hierarchy.
- Many of the scriptural rules of caste are thus designed to prevent the mixing of castes - rules ranging from marriage, food sharing and social interaction to occupation.
- The hierarchical ordering of castes is based on the distinction between 'purity' and 'pollution'.

- This is a division between something believed to be closer to the sacred (thus connoting ritual purity), and something believed to be distant from or opposed to the sacred, therefore considered ritually polluting.

- Castes that are considered ritually pure have high status, while those considered less pure or impure have low status.

Colonialism and Caste

- The present form of caste as a social institution has been shaped very strongly by both the colonial period as well as the rapid changes that have come about in independent India.

- Initially, the British administrators began by trying to understand the complexities of caste in an effort to learn how to govern the country efficiently.

- Some of these efforts took the shape of very methodical and intensive surveys and reports on the 'customs and manners' of various tribes and castes all over the country.

- The most important official effort to collect information on caste was through the census.

- The land revenue settlements and related arrangements and laws served to give legal recognition to the customary (caste-based) rights of the upper castes.

- These castes now became land owners in the modern sense rather than feudal classes with claims on the produce of the land, or claims to revenue or tribute of various kinds.

- At the other end of the scale, towards the end of the colonial period, the administration also took an interest in the welfare of downtrodden castes, referred to as the 'depressed classes' at that time.

- It was as part of these efforts that the Government of India Act of 1935 was passed which gave legal recognition to the lists or 'schedules' of castes and tribes marked out for special treatment by the state.

- This is how the terms 'Scheduled Tribes' and the 'Scheduled Castes' came into being. Castes at the bottom of the hierarchy that suffered severe discrimination, including all the so-called 'untouchable' castes, were included among the Scheduled Castes.

Caste in the Present

- Caste considerations had inevitably played a role in the mass mobilisations of the nationalist movement.

- Efforts to organise the "depressed classes" and particularly the untouchable castes predated the nationalist movement, having begun in the second half of the nineteenth century.

- This was an initiative taken from both ends of the caste spectrum - by upper caste progressive reformers as well as by members of the lower castes such as Mahatma Jotiba Phule and Babasaheb Ambedkar in western India, Ayyankali, Sri Narayana Guru, Iyotheedass and Periyar (E.V. Ramaswamy Naickar) in the South.

- Both Mahatma Gandhi and Babasaheb Ambedkar began organising protests against untouchability from the 1920s onwards.

- Anti-untouchability programmes became a significant part of the Congress agenda so that, by the time Independence was on the horizon, there was a broad agreement across the spectrum of the nationalist movement to abolish caste distinctions.

- Modern industry created all kinds of new jobs for which there were no caste rules.

- Urbanisation and the conditions of collective living in the cities made it difficult for the caste-segregated patterns of social interaction to survive.

- Recruitment to industrial jobs, whether in the textile mills of Mumbai (then Bombay), the jute mills of Kolkata (then Calcutta), or elsewhere, continued to be organised along caste and kinship-based lines.

- The middle men who recruited labour for factories tended to recruit them from their own caste and region so that particular departments or shop floors were often dominated by specific castes.

- 'Sanskritisation' refers to a process whereby members of a (usually middle or lower) caste attempt to raise their own social status by adopting the ritual, domestic and social practices of a caste (or castes) of higher status.

- Sanskritisation usually accompanies or follows a rise in the economic status of the caste attempting it, though it may also occur independently.

- 'Dominant caste' is a term used to refer to those castes which had a large population and were granted land rights by the partial land reforms effected after Independence.

- The intermediate castes became the 'dominant' castes in the country side and played a decisive role in regional politics and the agrarian economy. Examples of such dominant castes include the Yadavs of Bihar and Uttar Pradesh, the Vokkaligas of Karnataka, the Reddys and Khammas of Andhra Pradesh, the Marathas of Maharashtra, the Jats of Punjab, Haryana and Western Uttar Pradesh and the Patidars of Gujarat.

Changes in the caste system

- Economic educational resources
- Opportunities offered by rapid development
- Public education
- Professional education in science, technology, medicine and management
- Expansion of public sector jobs

Tribal Communities

- Tribe' is a modern term for communities that are very old, being among the oldest inhabitants of the sub-continent.
- Tribes in India have generally been defined in terms of what they were not.
- Tribes were communities that did not practice a religion with a written text; did not have a state or political form of the normal kind; did not have sharp class divisions; and, most important, they did not have caste and were neither Hindus nor peasants.

Classification of Tribes

- In terms of positive characteristics, tribes have been classified according to their 'permanent' and 'acquired' traits.

Permanent traits

- About 85% of the tribal population lives in 'middle India', a wide band stretching from Gujarat and Rajasthan in the west to West Bengal and Odisha in the east, with Madhya Pradesh, Jharkhand, Chattisgarh and parts of Maharashtra and Andhra Pradesh forming the heart of this region.
- Of the remaining 15%, over 11% is in the North Eastern states, leaving only a little over 3% living in the rest of India.
- North Eastern states have the highest concentrations, with all states, except Assam, having concentrations of more than 30%, and some, like Arunachal Pradesh, Meghalaya, Mizoram and Nagaland with more than 60% and upto 95% of tribal population.
- The ecological habitats covered includes hills, forests, rural plains and urban industrial areas.
- In terms of language, tribes are categorised into four categories. Two of them, Indo-Aryan and Dravidian, are shared by the rest of the Indian population as well, and tribes account for only about 1% of the former and about 3% of the latter.
- The other two language groups, the Austric and Tibeto-Burman, are primarily spoken by tribals, who account for all of the first and over 80% of the second group.

- In physical-racial terms, tribes are classified under the Negrito, Australoid, Mongoloid, Dravidian and Aryan categories.
- The biggest tribes are the Gonds, Bhils, Santhals, Oraons, Minas, Bodos and Mundas, all of whom are at least a million strong.
- The total population of tribes amounts to about 8.2% of the population of India, or about 84 million persons according to the 2001 Census.

Acquired traits

- Classifications based on acquired traits use two main criteria - mode of livelihood, and extent of incorporation into Hindu society - or a combination of the two.
- On the basis of livelihood, tribes can be categorised into fishermen, food gatherers and hunters, shifting cultivators, peasants and plantation and industrial workers.
- From the tribes' point of view, apart from the extent of assimilation, attitude towards Hindu society is also a major criterion, with differentiation between tribes that are positively inclined towards Hinduism and those who resist or oppose it.

Tribal Identity

- Tribal identities are formed by interactional process rather than any primordial (original, ancient) characteristics peculiar to tribes.
- The positive impact of successes - such as the achievement of statehood for Jharkhand and Chattisgarh after a long struggle - is moderated by continuing problems.
- Many of the states of the North-East, for example, have been living for decades under special laws that limit the civil liberties of citizens.
- Thus, citizens of states like Manipur or Nagaland don't have the same rights as other citizens of India because their states have been declared as 'disturbed areas'.
- Another significant development is the gradual emergence of an educated middle class among tribal communities.
- Two broad sets of issues have been most important in giving rise to tribal movements. These are issues relating to control over vital economic resources like land and specially forests, and issues relating to matters of ethnic-cultural identity. The two can often go together, but with differentiation of tribal society they may also diverge.

Family and Kinship

- The structure of the family can be studied both as a social institution in itself and also in its relationship to other social institutions of society.

- In itself a family can be defined as nuclear or extended. It can be male-headed or female-headed. The line of descent can be matrilineal or patrilineal.

- The migration of men from the villages of the Himalayan region can lead to an unusual proportion of women-headed families in the village. Or the work schedules of young parents in the software industry in India may lead to increasing number of grandparents moving in as care-givers to young grandchildren.

- It is evident from the kind of changes that take place that not only have family structures changed, but cultural ideas, norms and values also change. These changes are however not so easy to bring about.

Nuclear and Extended Family

- A nuclear family consists of only one set of parents and their children.

- An extended family (commonly known as the 'joint family') can take different forms, but has more than one couple, and often more than two generations, living together.

- This could be a set of brothers with their individual families, or an elderly couple with their sons and grandsons and their respective families. The extended family often is seen as symptomatic of India.

Diverse Forms of Family

- With regard to the rule of residence, some societies are matrilocal in their marriage and family customs while others are patrilocal.

- In matrilocal, the newly married couple stays with the woman's parents, whereas in the second case the couple lives with the man's parents.

- With regard to the rules of inheritance, matrilineal societies pass on property from mother to daughter while patrilineal societies do so from father to son.

- A patriarchal family structure exists where the men exercise authority and dominance, and matriarchy where the women play a similarly dominant role.

- However, matriarchy, unlike patriarchy has been a theoretical rather than an empirical concept. There is no historical or anthropological evidence of matriarchy i.e., societies where women exercise dominance.

- However, there do exist matrilineal societies, i.e., societies where women inherit property from their mothers but do not exercise control over it, nor are they the decision makers in public affairs.

Exercise

1. **Assertion (A):** Caste refers to a broad institutional arrangement in Indian languages.

   Reason (R): Indian society is divided into four-fold division called varna which distinct people on the basis of color.
   - (a) Both A and R are true and R is the correct explanation of A.
   - (b) Both A and R are true but R is not the correct explanation of A.
   - (c) A is true and R is false.
   - (d) A is false and R is true.

2. Which of the following are known as panchamans in Indian society?
   - I.   Shudras
   - II. Slaves
   - III. Foreigners
   - (a) I and II
   - (b) II and III
   - (c) I and III
   - (d) I, II and III

3. Caste system in India is recognized through which of the following factors?
   - I.   Endogamy
   - II. Hierarchy
   - III. Traditional occupation
   - (a) I and II
   - (b) I and III
   - (c) II and III
   - (d) All of the above

4. Which of the following set of principles are followed in caste system in India?
   - (a) Differences and separation and wholism and hierarchy
   - (b) Division of society into castes and jatis
   - (c) Varna system and jatis
   - (d) Endogamy and hierarchical nature of society

5. The hierarchical ordering of caste is based on which of the following disctinction?
   - (a) Castes and sub-castes
   - (b) Four-fold division of society
   - (c) Purity and pollution
   - (d) Individual existence of castes

6. The present form of caste as a social institution has been shaped due to -
   - (a) Colonialism and rapid changes post-independence
   - (b) Sub-categorization of caste
   - (c) Hierarchical nature of society
   - (d) Untouchability

7. British administration tried to understand the caste complexities through which of the following ways?
   - (a) Categorization of labors on the basis of castes
   - (b) Methodical and intensive surveys
   - (c) Imposition of land revenue
   - (d) Economic status of population

8. **Assertion (A):** Caste system of today is more a product of colonialism than of ancient Indian tradition.

   Reason (R): Colonial government put efforts to understand the caste complexities to provide efficient governance.
   - (a) Both A and R are true and R is the correct explanation of A.
   - (b) Both A and R are true but R is not the correct explanation of A.
   - (c) A is true and R is false.
   - (d) A is false and R is true.

9. During colonial period, the legal recognition to the customary (caste-based) rights of the upper castes had been given through which of the following way?
   - (a) Census
   - (b) Caste-based surveys
   - (c) Land revenue settlement
   - (d) Establishment of industry

10. Which of the following act gave legal recognition to the 'schedules' of castes and tribes for special treatment?
    - (a) Govt. of India Act 1909
    - (b) Govt. of India Act 1919
    - (c) Indian Independence Act, 1947
    - (d) Govt. of India Act, 1935

11. Which of the following leaders took initiative to break the taboo of caste system?
    - I.   Ayyankali
    - II. Sri Narayan Guru
    - III. Iyotheedass
    - (a) I and III
    - (b) II and III
    - (c) I and II
    - (d) All of the above

12. Societies, where women inherit property from their mothers but do not exercise control over it, is known as -

(a) Matrilineal   (b) Matrilocal

(c) Matriarchal   (d) Patriarchal

13. Assertion (A): Initiative to organize "depressed classes" taken by both upper and lower caste leaders.

Reason (R): By the time Independence was on the horizon, there was a broad agreement across the spectrum of the nationalist movement to abolish caste distinctions.

(a) Both A and R are true and R is the correct explanation of A.

(b) Both A and R are true but R is not the correct explanation of A.

(c) A is true and R is false.

(d) A is false and R is true.

14. During colonial period, why recruitment to industrial jobs in the textile mills of Mumbai, the jute mills of Kolkata or elsewhere continued to organize along caste and kinship-based lines?

(a) Shortage of skilled labors among upper caste

(b) Lack of education

(c) Create dominance of specific caste

(d) Urbanization

15. In the sociology, 'dominant caste' refers to -

I. Large population of particular caste

II. Land rights granted post-independence

III. Intermediate castes

(a) I and II   (b) II and III

(c) I and III   (d) All of the above

16. 85% of tribal population lives in which of the following region of India?

(a) North-Eastern states

(b) Central India

(c) Bihar and Jharkhand

(d) Middle India

17. Tribes are categorized into which of the following set of languages?

I. Indo-Aryan and Dravidian

II. Austric and Tibeto-Burman

III. Dravidian and Austric

(a) I and II   (b) II and III

(c) I and III   (d) All of the above

18. Basket making and oil pressing is the occupation of which of the tribal group?

(a) Gonds   (b) Ho and Munda

(c) Birhors   (d) Santhals

19. The tribal movement in India has increased due to -

(a) Atrocities of non-tribals

(b) Control over vital economic resources and ethnic-cultural identity

(c) Migration of tribal population in the search of good education

(d) Loss of natural vegetation

20. The unusual proportion of women-headed families are found in village, the reason is -

(a) Migration of men from Himalayan region

(b) Feminization of agriculture

(c) Allotment of government schemes benefits to women

(d) Education facilities and employment

Answer Keys

1. (b) **2.** (b) **3.** (d) **4.** (a) **5.** (c) **6.** (a) **7.** (b) **8.** (a) **9.** (c) **10.** (d)

11. (d) **12.** (a) **13.** (b) **14.** (c) **15.** (d) **16.** (d) **17.** (a) **18.** (c) **19.** (b) **20.** (a)

CHAPTER 4

The Market as a Social Institution

Sociological Perspectives On Markets And The Economy

- Adam Smith, in his book, The Wealth of Nations, attempted to understand the market economy that was just emerging at that time.

- Smith argued that the market economy is made up of a series of individual exchanges or transactions, which automatically create a functioning and ordered system.

- There seems to be some sort of an unseen force at work that converts what is good for each individual into what is good for society. This unseen force was called 'the invisible hand' by Adam Smith.

- Smith argued that the capitalist economy is driven by individual self-interest, and works best when individual buyers and sellers make rational decisions that serve their own interests.

- Smith used the idea of the 'invisible hand' to argue that society overall benefits when individuals pursue their own self-interest in the market, because it stimulates the economy and creates more wealth.

- For this reason, Smith supported the idea of a 'free market', that is, a market free from all kinds of regulation whether by the state or otherwise. This economic philosophy was also given the name laissez-faire, a French phrase that means 'leave alone' or 'let it be'.

- Sociologists view markets as social institutions that are constructed in culturally specific ways. For example, markets are often controlled or organised by particular social groups or classes, and have specific connections to other institutions, social processes and structures.

- Sociologists often express this idea by saying that economies are socially 'embedded'. This is illustrated by two examples, one of a weekly tribal haat, and the other of a 'traditional business community' and its trading networks in colonial India.

Tribal Market

- The weekly haat is a common sight in rural and even urban India. In hilly and forested areas (especially those inhabited by adivasis), where settlements are far-flung, roads and communications poor, and the economy relatively undeveloped, the weekly market is the major institution for the exchange of goods as well as for social intercourse.

- A 'market' for tribal labour developed during the colonial period. Due to all these changes, local tribal economies became linked into wider markets, usually with very negative consequences for local people.

- The weekly market as a social institution, the links between the local tribal economy and the outside, and the exploitative economic relationships between adivasis and others, are illustrated by a study of a weekly market in Bastar district.

- The major goods that are exchanged in the market are manufactured goods (such as jewellery and trinkets, pots and knives), non-local foods (such as salt and haldi (turmeric)), local food and agricultural produce and manufactured items (such as bamboo baskets), and forest produce (such as tamarind and oil-seeds).

Caste-Based Markets And Trading Networks In Pre-colonial And Colonial India

- Economic transformation was thought to have begun only with the advent of colonialism

- Under colonialism and in the early post-independence period, the penetration of the commercial money economy into local agrarian economies, and their incorporation into wider networks of exchange, was thought to have brought about radical social and economic changes in rural and urban society.

- Various kinds of non-market exchange systems (such as the 'jajmani system') did exist in many villages and regions, even during the precolonial period villages were incorporated into wider networks of exchange through which agricultural products and other goods circulated.

- India was a major manufacturer and exporter of handloom cloth (both ordinary cotton and luxury silks), as well as the source of many other goods (such as spices) that were in great demand in the global market, especially in Europe.

- The pre-colonial India had well-organised manufacturing centres as well as indigenous merchant groups, trading networks, and banking systems that enabled trade to take place within India, and between India and the rest of the world.

- These traditional trading communities or castes had their own systems of banking and credit. For instance, an important instrument of exchange and credit was the hundi, or bill of exchange (like a credit note), which allowed merchants to engage in long-distance trade.

- The Nattukottai Chettiars (or Nakarattars) of Tamil Nadu, provide an interesting illustration of how these indigenous trading networks were organised and worked.

Colonialism And The Emergence Of New Markets

- The advent of colonialism in India produced major upheavals in the economy, causing disruptions in production, trade, and agriculture.

- In the colonial era India began to be more fully linked to the world capitalist economy.

- Before being colonised by the British, India was a major supplier of manufactured goods to the world market.

- After colonisation, she became a source of raw materials and agricultural products and a consumer of manufactured goods, both largely for the benefit of industrialising England.

Understanding Capitalism As A Social System

- One of the founders of modern sociology, Karl Marx, was also a critic of modern capitalism.

- Marx understood capitalism as a system of commodity production, or production for the market, through the use of wage labour. As you have already learned, Marx wrote that all economic systems are also social systems.

- Each mode of production consists of particular relations of production, which in turn give rise to a specific class structure.

- He emphasised that the economy does not consist of things (goods circulating in the market), but is made up of relations between people who are connected to one another through the process of production.

- Under the capitalist mode of production, labour itself becomes a commodity, because workers must sell their labour power in the market to earn a wage.

- This gives rise to two basic classes - capitalists, who own the means of production (such as the factories), and workers, who sell their labour to the capitalists.

- The capitalist class is able to profit from this system by paying the workers less than the value of what they actually produce, and so extracting surplus value from their labour.

Commoditisation And Consumption

- Commodification occurs when things that were earlier not traded in the market become commodities. For instance, labour or skills become things that can be bought and sold.

- In earlier times, social skills such as good manners and etiquette were imparted mainly through the family.

- Another important feature of capitalist society is that consumption becomes more and more important, not just for economic reasons but because it has symbolic meaning. In modern societies, consumption is an important way in which social distinctions are created and communicated.

- The consumer conveys a message about his or her socioeconomic status or cultural preferences by buying and displaying certain goods, and companies try to sell their goods by appealing to symbols of status or culture.

- One of sociology's founders, Max Weber, was among the first to point out that the goods that people buy and use are closely related to their status in society. He coined the term status symbol to describe this relationship.

- Weber also wrote about how classes and status groups are differentiated on the basis of their lifestyles.

- Consumption is one aspect of lifestyle, but it also includes the way you decorate your home and the way you dress, your leisure activities, and many other aspects of daily life. Sociologists study consumption patterns and lifestyles because of their cultural and social significance in modern life.

Globalisation - Interlinking Of Local, Regional, National And International Markets

- Since the late 1980s, India has entered a new era in its economic history, following the change in economic policy from one of statel-ed development to liberalisation.

- This shift also ushered in the era of globalisation, a period in which the world is becoming increasingly interconnected - not only economically but also culturally and politically.

- The term globalisation includes a number of trends, especially the increase in international movement of commodities, money, information, and people, as well as the development of technology (such as in computers, telecommunications, and transport) and other infrastructure to allow this movement.

- A central feature of globalisation is the increasing extension and integration of markets around the world.

- The software services industries and business process outsourcing (BPO) industries (such as call centres) are some of the major avenues through which India is getting connected to the global economy.

- Companies based in India provide low-cost services and labour to customers located in the developed countries of the West.

- Under globalisation, not only money and goods, but also people, cultural products, and images circulate rapidly around the world, enter new circuits of exchange, and create new markets.

Debate On Liberalisation - Market Versus State

- Liberalisation includes a range of policies such as the privatisation of public sector enterprises (selling government-owned companies to private companies); loosening of government regulations on capital, labour, and trade; a reduction in tariffs and import duties so that foreign goods can be imported more easily; and allowing easier access for foreign companies to set up industries in India.

- Another word for such changes is marketisation, or the use of markets or market-based processes (rather than government regulations or policies) to solve social, political, or economic problems.

- These include relaxation or removal of economic controls (deregulation), privatisation of industries, and removing government controls over wages and prices.

- Increasing foreign investment is supposed to help economic growth and employment. The privatisation of public companies is supposed to increase their efficiency and reduce the government's burden of running these companies. However, the impact of liberalisation has been mixed.

- Some sectors of Indian industry (like software and information technology) or agriculture (like fish or fruit) may benefit from access to a global market, but other sectors (like automobiles, electronics or oilseeds) will lose because they cannot compete with foreign producers.

- Indian farmers are now exposed to competition from farmers in other countries because import of agricultural products is allowed.

- Liberalisation is against this kind of government interference in markets, so support prices and subsidies are reduced or withdrawn. This means that many farmers are not able to make a decent living from agriculture.

- Similarly, small manufacturers have been exposed to global competition as foreign goods and brands have entered the market, and some have not been able to compete.

- The privatisation or closing of public sector industries has led to loss of employment in some sectors, and to growth of unorganised sector employment at the expense of the organised sector. This is not good for workers because the organised sector generally offers better paid and more regular or permanent jobs.

Exercise

1. Adam Smith, in his book, 'Wealth of Nations', which type of economy has emerged?

(a) Social economy   (b) Political economy

(c) Market economy   (d) Capitalist economy

2. Assertion (A): Sociologists view markets as social institutions that are constructed in culturally specific ways.

Reason (R): As sociologists believe that economies are socially 'embedded'.

(a) Both A and R are true and R is the correct explanation of A

(b) Both A and R are true but R is not the correct explanation of A

(c) A is true and R is false

(d) A is false and R is true

3. Adam Smith used the idea of 'invisible hand' in the context of -

(a) Benefits of society through pursuing of self interest

(b) Capitalist market economy

(c) Investment of money in the economy

(d) Opening up of the new markets

4. Assertion (A): In rural India, there are specialised markets that take place at less frequent intervals.

Reason (R): Markets provide a link to regional economy to wider national economy.

(a) Both A and R are true and R is the correct explanation of A

(b) Both A and R are true but R is not the correct explanation of A

(c) A is true and R is false

(d) A is false and R is true

5. Tribal areas were 'opened up' by building roads and 'pacifying' the local people due to which of the following reason?

(a) To provide connectivity to the market to sell the local produce

(b) To provide better road connectivity supporting migration of people

(c) To exploit the rich forest and mineral resources of these areas

(d) To implement the modern thoughts in the tribal society

6. Which of the changes had been accounted in the tribal society during colonial period?

I. Recruitment at plantation sites as laborers

II. Markets were established for tribal labors

III. Loss of lands of tribals

(a) I and II   (b) II and III

(c) I and III   (d) All of the above

7. Jajmani system has existed in many villages and region during precolonial period, it is -

(a) Market economy

(b) Non-market economy

(c) Trade exchange

(d) Door-to-door service

Read the following passage and answer the questions 8, 9 and 10

The Nattukottai Chettiars (or Nakarattars) of Tamil Nadu, provide an interesting illustration of how these indigenous trading networks were organised and worked. A study of this community during the colonial period shows how its banking and trade activities were deeply embedded in the social organisation of the community. The structures of caste, kinship, and family were oriented towards commercial activity, and business activity was carried out within these social structures. As in most 'traditional' merchant communities, Nakarattar banks were basically joint family firms, so that the structure of the business firm was the same as that of the family. Similarly, trading and banking activities were organised through caste and kinship relationships. For instance, their extensive caste-based social networks allowed Chettiar merchants to expand their activities into Southeast Asia and Ceylon. In one view, the economic activities of the Nakarattars represented a kind of indigenous capitalism. This interpretation raises the question of whether there are, or were, forms of 'capitalism' apart from those that arose in Europe (Rudner 1994).

8. As per the given passage, which of the following is not true for Chettiars?

(a) Commercial activity was carried out with other castes

(b) They ran banks as join family firm

(c) They established indigenous capitalism

(d) They expanded their activities in neigbouring countries

9. What allowed Chettiar merchants to expand their activities into Southeast Asia and Ceylon?

   (a) Their business model

   (b) Joint family firms

   (c) Extensive caste based social network

   (d) Profitable trade

10. The economic activities of Chettiars are represented as a kind of indigenous capitalism, why?

    (a) Due to their social network

    (b) Their banking and trade activities were embedded in social organization

    (c) Caste, kinship and family oriented towards commercial activities

    (d) Expansion of trade

11. **Assertion (A):** Nakarattar banking system resembled an economist's model of Western-style banking systems.

    Reason (R): They loaned and deposited money with one another in caste-defined social relationships based on business territory, residential location, descent, marriage, and common cult membership.

    (a) Both A and R are true and R is the correct explanation of A

    (b) Both A and R are true but R is not the correct explanation of A

    (c) A is true and R is false

    (d) A is false and R is true

12. Why there is a complex relationship between caste status or identity, and caste practices in India?

    (a) Non-availability of caste rule

    (b) Due to historical caste structure

    (c) Inclusion of Vaishyas in upper class fold

    (d) Inclusion of business class into Vaishya community

13. The community which has benefitted during colonial period includes shopkeepers and small traders in the bazaars of towns throughout the country is -

    (a) Baniyas

    (b) Chettiars

    (c) Marwaris

    (d) Vaishyas

Read the following passage and answer the questions 14, 15 and 16

One of the founders of modern sociology, Karl Marx, was also a critic of modern capitalism. Marx understood capitalism as a system of commodity production, or production for the market, through the use of wage labour. As you have already learned, Marx wrote that all economic systems are also social systems. Each mode of production consists of particular relations of production, which in turn give rise to a specific class structure. He emphasised that the economy does not consist of things (goods circulating in the market), but is made up of relations between people who are connected to one another through the process of production. Under the capitalist mode of production, labour itself becomes a commodity, because workers must sell their labour power in the market to earn a wage. This gives rise to two basic classes - capitalists, who own the means of production (such as the factories), and workers, who sell their labour to the capitalists. The capitalist class is able to profit from this system by paying the workers less than the value of what they actually produce, and so extracting surplus value from their labour. Marx's theory of capitalist economy and society provided the inspiration for numerous theories and debates about the nature of capitalism throughout the nineteenth and twentieth centuries.

14. Capitalism was understood by Karl Marx as -

    (a) Production of commodity

    (b) Use of labor

    (c) Production of commodity by using labor

    (d) Exploitation of labor

15. Karl Marx considered Economic system as -

    (a) Capitalist economic system

    (b) Social system

    (c) Commodification

    (d) Use of labor

16. As per Marx, through which way capitalist class earn profit through labor which production of commodity?

    (a) Exploitation of economic resources

    (b) Excessive use of labor

    (c) Investment of more profit into business

    (d) Paying less to the workers than the value of actual production by them

17. Commodification occurs when things that were earlier not traded in the market become commodities. What is the commodity in Marx theory?

(a) Wage labors

(b) Production of commodity

(c) Capital money

(d) Raw materials

18. The globalisation of the Indian economy has been due primarily to the policy of liberalisation that was started in the late 1980s. Which of the following includes the features of liberalization?

I. Privatization of PSUs

II. Tightening the government regulation on trade

III. Access to foreign companies to set up establishments

(a) I and II   (b) I and III

(c) II and III   (d) All of the above

19. Indian farmers who are now exposed to competition from farmers in other countries as import of agricultural products is allowed. This become possible due to -

(a) Globalization

(b) Commodification

(c) Privatization

(d) Liberalization

20. Indian agriculture was protected from the world market by support prices and subsidies. Government gives such support due to-

(a) Increment of profit in agriculture

(b) Ensuring minimum income to the farmers

(c) Protecting farmers from the crop damage

(d) Increase investment in the farming

Answer Keys

1. (c)	**2.** (a)	**3.** (a)	**4.** (a)	**5.** (c)	**6.** (d)	**7.** (b)	**8.** (a)	**9.** (c)	**10.** (b)
11. (d)	**12.** (b)	**13.** (c)	**14.** (c)	**15.** (b)	**16.** (d)	**17.** (a)	**18.** (b)	**19.** (d)	**20.** (b)

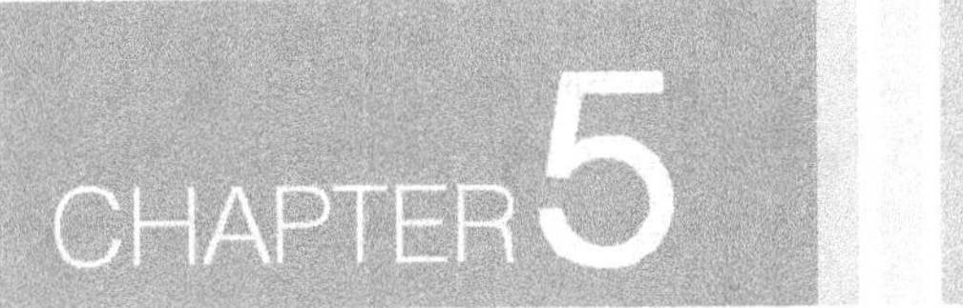

Patterns of Social Inequality and Exclusion

What Is Social About Social Inequality And Exclusion?

- Social inequality and exclusion are social because they are not about individuals but about groups.

- They are social in the sense that they are not economic, although there is usually a strong link between social and economic inequality.

- They are systematic and structured as there is a definite pattern to social inequalities.

Social Inequalities

- The social resources can be divided into three forms of capital - economic capital in the form of material assets and income; cultural capital such as educational qualifications and status; and social capital in the form of networks of contacts and social associations.

- Patterns of unequal access to social resources are commonly called social inequality.

- Sociologists use the term social stratification to refer to a system by which categories of people in a society are ranked in a hierarchy. This hierarchy then shapes people's identity and experiences, their relations with others, as well as their access to resources and opportunities.

- Three key principles help explain social stratification:

  - **Social stratification is a characteristic of society, not simply a function of individual differences:** Social stratification is a society-wide system that unequally distributes social resources among categories of people.

  - **Social stratification persists over generations:** It is closely linked to the family and to the inheritance of social resources from one generation to the next. A person's social position is ascribed. That is, children assume the social positions of their parents.

  - **Social stratification is supported by patterns of belief, or ideology:** Justification of caste system in terms of the opposition of purity and pollution, with the Brahmins designated as the most superior and Dalits as the most inferior by virtue of their birth and occupation.

- Prejudices refer to pre-conceived opinions or attitudes held by members of one group towards another.

- Prejudices are often grounded in stereotypes, fixed and inflexible characterisations of a group of people. Stereotypes are often applied to ethnic and racial groups and to women.

- If prejudice describes attitudes and opinions, discrimination refers to actual behaviour towards another group or individual. Discrimination can be seen in practices that disqualify members of one group from opportunities open to others, as when a person is refused a job because of their gender or religion.

Social Exclusion

- Social exclusion refers to ways in which individuals may become cut off from full involvement in the wider society.

- It focuses attention on a broad range of factors that prevent individuals or groups from having opportunities open to the majority of the population.

- India like most societies has been marked by acute practices of social discrimination and exclusion

- It is important to note that social exclusion is involuntary - that is, exclusion is practiced regardless of the wishes of those who are excluded.

- Social exclusion is sometimes wrongly justified by the same logic - it is said that the excluded group itself does not wish to participate. The truth of such an argument is not obvious when exclusion is preventing access to something desirable.

The Caste System As A Discriminatory System

- The caste system is a distinct Indian social institution that legitimises and enforces practices of discrimination against people born into particular castes.

- These practices of discrimination are humiliating, exclusionary and exploitative.

- Historically, the caste system classified people by their occupation and status. Every caste was associated with an occupation, which meant that persons born into a particular caste were also 'born into' the occupation associated with their caste - they had no choice.

- In strict scriptural terms, social and economic status were supposed to be sharply separated. For example, the ritually highest caste - the Brahmins - were not supposed to amass wealth, and were subordinated to the secular power of kings and rulers belonging to the Kshatriya castes.

- However, in actual historical practice economic and social status tended to coincide. There was thus a fairly close correlation between social (i.e. caste) status and economic status - the 'high' castes were almost invariably of high economic status, while the 'low' castes were almost always of low economic status.

Untouchability

- 'Untouchability' is an extreme and particularly vicious aspect of the caste system that prescribes stringent social sanctions against members of castes located at the bottom of the purity-pollution scale.

- It is important to emphasise that the three main dimensions of untouchability - namely, exclusion, humiliation-subordination and exploitation - are all equally important in defining the phenomenon.

- Dalits experience forms of exclusion that are unique and not practised against other groups - for instance, being prohibited from sharing drinking water sources or participating in collective religious worship, social ceremonies and festivals.

- The performance of publicly visible acts of (self) humiliation and subordination is an important part of the practice of untouchability.

- Moreover, untouchability is almost always associated with economic exploitation of various kinds, most commonly through the imposition of forced, unpaid (or under-paid) labour, or the confiscation of property.

- Finally, untouchability is a pan-Indian phenomenon, although its specific forms and intensity vary considerably across regions and socio-historical contexts.

- The so-called 'untouchables' have been referred to collectively by many names over the centuries. Mahatma Gandhi had popularised the term 'Harijan' (literally, children of God) in the 1930s to counter the pejorative charge carried by caste names.

- However, the ex-untouchable communities and their leaders have coined another term, 'Dalit', which is now the generally accepted term for referring to these groups. In Indian languages, the term Dalit literally means 'downtrodden' and conveys the sense of an oppressed people.

- It was neither coined by Dr. Ambedkar nor frequently used by him, the term certainly resonates with his philosophy and the movement for empowerment that he led.

- The Dalit Panthers, a radical group that emerged in western India during that time, used the term to assert their identity as part of their struggle for rights and dignity.

State And Non-State Initiatives Addressing Caste And Tribe Discrimination

- The Indian state has had special programmes for the Scheduled Tribes and Scheduled Castes since even before Independence.

- The 'Schedules' listing the castes and tribes recognised as deserving of special treatment because of the massive discrimination practiced against them were drawn up in 1935, by the British Indian government.

- Among the most significant additions is the extension of special programmes to the Other Backward Classes (OBCs) since the early 1990s.

- The most important state initiative attempting to compensate for past and present caste discrimination is the one popularly known as 'reservations'.

- This involves the setting aside of some places or 'seats' for members of the Scheduled Castes and Tribes in different spheres of public life. These include reservation of seats in the State and Central legislatures (i.e., state assemblies, Lok Sabha and Rajya Sabha); reservation of jobs in government service across all departments and public sector companies; and reservation of seats in educational institutions.

- The proportion of reserved seats is equal to the percentage share of the Scheduled Castes and Tribes in the total population. But for the OBCs this proportion is decided differently.

- The Caste Disabilities Removal Act of 1850 disallowed the curtailment of rights of citizens due solely to change of religion or caste.

- The most recent such law was the Constitution Amendment (Ninety Third Amendment) Act of 2005, which became law on 23rd January 2006. Coincidentally, both the 1850 law and the 2006 amendment related to education.

- The 93rd Amendment is for introducing reservation for the Other Backward Classes in institutions of higher education, while the 1850 Act was used to allow entry of Dalits to government schools.

- The Constitution abolished untouchability (Article 17) and introduced the reservation provisions mentioned above.

- The 1989 Prevention of Atrocities Act revised and strenthened the legal provisions punishing acts of violence or humiliation against Dalits and adivasis.

- State action alone cannot ensure social change. In any case, no social group howsoever weak or oppressed is only a victim.

- Dalits too have been increasingly active on the political, agitational, and cultural fronts.

- From the pre-Independence struggles and movements launched by people like Jyotiba Phule, Iyotheedas, Periyar, Ambedkar and other to contemporary political organisations like the Bahujan Samaj Party in Uttar Pradesh or the Dalit Sangharsh Samiti of Karnataka, Dalit political assertion has come a long way.

- Dalits have also made significant contributions to literature in several Indian languages, specially Marathi, Kannada, Tamil, Telugu and Hindi.

The Other Backward Classes

- The Constitution of India recognises the possibility that there may be groups other than the Scheduled Tribes and Scheduled Castes who suffer from social disadvantages.

- These groups - which need not be based on caste alone, but generally are identified by caste - were described as the 'socially and educationally backward classes'. This is the constitutional basis of the popular term 'Other Backward Classes' (OBCs).

- The OBCs are a much more diverse group than the Dalits or adivasis.

- The first government of independent India under Jawaharlal Nehru appointed a commission to look into measures for the welfare of the OBCs.

- The First Backward Classes Commission headed by Kaka Kalelkar submitted its report in 1953. But the political climate at the time led to the report being sidelined.

- From the mid-fifties, the OBC issue became a regional affair pursued at the state rather than the central level.

- The southern states had a long history of backward caste political agitation that had started in the early twentieth century.

- Because of these powerful social movements, policies to address the problems of the OBCs were in place long before they were discussed in most northern states.

- The OBC issue returned to the central level in the late 1970s after the Emergency when the Janata Party came to power.

- The Second Backward Classes Commission headed by B.P. Mandal was appointed at this time.

- However, it was only in 1990, when the central government decided to implement the ten-year old Mandal Commission report, that the OBC issue became a major one in national politics.

- The politicisation of the OBCs allows them to convert their large numbers - recent surveys show that they are about 41% of the national population - into political influence.

- This was not possible at the national level before, as shown by the sidelining of the Kalelkar Commission report, and the neglect of the Mandal Commission report.

Adivasi Struggles

- The jana or tribes were believed to be 'people of the forest' whose distinctive habitat in the hill and forest areas shaped their economic, social and political attributes.

- Tribal groups have had long and close association with Hindu society and culture, making the boundaries between 'tribe' and 'caste' quite porous.

- Today, barring the North-Eastern states, there are no areas of the country that are inhabited exclusively by tribal people; there are only areas of tribal concentration.

- Since the middle of the nineteenth century, non-tribals have moved into the tribal districts of central India, while tribal people from the same districts have migrated to plantations, mines, factories and other places of employment.

- From the late nineteenth century onwards, the colonial government reserved most forest tracts for its own use, severing the rights that adivasis had long exercised to use the forest for gathering produce and for shifting cultivation. Forests were now to be protected for maximising timber production.

- Denied access to forests and land for cultivation, adivasis were forced to either use the forests illegally (and be harassed and prosecuted as 'encroachers' and thieves) or migrate in search of wage labour.

- Firstly, after the Independence of India in 1947, the government monopoly over forests continued.

- Secondly, the policy of capital-intensive industrialisation adopted by the Indian government required mineral resources and power-generation capacities which were concentrated in Adivasi areas.

- Adivasi lands were rapidly acquired for new mining and dam projects. In the process, millions of adivasis were displaced without any appropriate compensation or rehabilitation

- It was justified in the name of 'national development' and 'economic growth', these policies were also a form of internal colonialism, subjugating adivasis and alienating the resources upon which they depended.

- Projects such as the Sardar Sarovar dam on the river Narmada in western India and the Polavaram dam on the river Godavari in Andhra Pradesh displace hundreds of thousands of adivasis, driving them to greater destitution.

- Like the term Dalit, the term Adivasi connotes political awareness and the assertion of rights. Literally meaning 'original inhabitants', the term was coined in the 1930s as part of the struggle against the intrusion by the colonial government and outside settlers and moneylenders.

- Being Adivasi is about shared experiences of the loss of forests, the alienation of land, repeated displacements since Independence in the name of 'development projects' and much more.

Struggle For Women's Equality And Rights

- Because of the obvious biological and physical differences between men and women, gender inequality is often treated as natural.

- Gender is thus also a form of social inequality and exclusion like caste and class, but with its own specific features.

- The women's question arose in modern India as part of the nineteenth century middle class social reform movements.

- They are often termed as middle class reform movements because many of these reformers were from the newly emerging western educated Indian middle class.

- They were often at once inspired by the democratic ideals of the modern west and by a deep pride in their own democratic traditions of the past.

- The anti-sati campaign led by Raja Rammohun Roy in Bengal, the widow remarriage movement in the Bombay Presidency where Ranade was one of the leading reformers, from Jyotiba Phule's simultaneous attack on caste and gender oppression, and from the social reform movement in Islam led by Sir Syed Ahmed Khan.

- Raja Rammohun Roy's attempts to reform society, religion and the status of women can be taken as the starting point of nineteenth century social reform in Bengal.

- A decade before establishing the Brahmo Samaj in 1828, Roy undertook the campaign against "sati" which was the first women's issue to receive public attention.

- Rammohun Roy's ideas represented a curious mixture of Western rationality and an assertion of Indian traditionality.

- Rammohun thus attacked the practice of sati on the basis of both appeals to humanitarian and natural rights doctrines as well as Hindu shastras.

- The deplorable and unjust treatment of the Hindu upper caste widows was a major issue taken up by the social reformers.

- Ranade used the writings of scholars such as Bishop Joseph Butler whose 'Analogy of Religion' and 'Three Sermons on Human Nature' dominated the moral philosophy syllabus of Bombay University in the 1860s.

- At the same time, M.G. Ranade's writings entitled the 'The Texts of the Hindu Law' on the 'Lawfulness of the Remarriage of Widows and Vedic Authorities for Widow Marriage' elaborated the shastric sanction for remarriage of widows.

- While Ranade and Rammohun Roy belonged to one kind of nineteenth century upper caste and middle class social reformers, Jotiba Phule came from a socially excluded caste and his attack was directed against both caste and gender discrimination.

- He founded the Satyashodak Samaj with its primary emphasis on "truth seeking". Phule's first practical social reform efforts were to aid the two groups considered lowest in traditional Brahmin culture: women and untouchables.

- A similar trend of drawing upon both modern western ideas as well as the sacred texts characterised Sir Syed Ahmed Khan's efforts to reform Muslim society. He wanted girls to be educated, but within the precincts of their homes. Like Dayanand Saraswati of the Arya Samaj, he stood for women's education but sought for a curriculum that included instruction in religious principles, training in the arts of housekeeping and handicrafts and rearing of children.
- **Stree Purush Tulana** (or Comparison of Men and Women) was written by a Maharashtrian housewife, Tarabai Shinde, as a protest against the double standards of a male dominated society.
- A young Brahmin widow had been sentenced to death by the courts for killing her newborn baby because it was illegitimate, but no effort had been made to identify or punish the man who had fathered the baby. Stree Purush Tulana created quite a stir when it was published.
- **Begum Rokeya Sakhawat Hossain** - was born in a well-to-do Bengali Muslim family, and was lucky to have a husband who was very liberal in outlook and encouraged her education first in Urdu and later in Bengali and English.
  - She was already a successful author in Urdu and Bengali when she wrote Sultana's Dream to test her abilities in English.
  - This remarkable short story is probably the earliest example of science fiction writing in India, and among the first by a woman author anywhere in the world.
  - In her dream, Sultana visits a magical country where the gender roles are reversed.
  - Men are confined to the home and observe 'purdah' while women are busy scientists vying with each other at inventing devices that will control the clouds and regulate rain, and machines that fly or 'air-cars'.
- In 1931, the Karachi Session of the Indian National Congress issued a declaration on the Fundamental Rights of Citizenship in India whereby it committed itself to women's equality. The declaration reads as follows:
  1. All citizens are equal before the law, irrespective of religion, caste, creed or sex.
  2. No disability attaches to any citizen, by reason of his or her religion, caste, creed or sex, in regard to public employment, office of power or honour, and in the exercise of any trade or calling.
  3. The franchise shall be on the basis of universal adult suffrage.
  4. Woman shall have the right to vote, to represent and the right to hold public offices. (Report of the Sub-Committee, 'Woman's Role in Planned Economy'.

Women's Struggle for Rights after Independence

- Two decades after Independence, women's issues re-emerged in the 1970s. In the nineteenth century reform movements, the emphasis had been on the backward aspects of tradition like sati, child marriage, or the ill treatment of widows.
- Two decades after Independence, women's issues re-emerged in the 1970s. In the nineteenth century reform movements, the emphasis had been on the backward aspects of tradition like sati, child marriage, or the ill treatment of widows. In the 1970s, the emphasis was on 'modern' issues - the rape of women in police custody, dowry murders, the representation of women in popular media, and the gendered consequences of unequal development.
- The law was a major site for reform in the 1980s and after, specially when it was discovered that many laws of concern to women had not been changed since the 19th century.
- The sharp fall in the child sex ratio and the implicit social bias against the girl child represents one of the new challenges of gender inequality.

The Struggles of The Disabled

- The differently abled are not 'disabled' only because they are physically or mentally 'impaired' but also because society is built in a manner that does not cater to their needs.
- The very term 'disabled' is significant because it draws attention to the fact that public perception of the 'disabled' needs to be questioned. Here are some common features central to the public perception of 'diability' all over the world -
  - Disability is understood as a biological given.
  - Whenever a disabled person is confronted with problems, it is taken for granted that the problems originate from her/his impairment.
  - The disabled person is seen as a victim.
  - Disability is supposed to be linked with the disabled individual's self-perception.
  - The very idea of disability suggests that they are in need of help
- In India labels such as 'disability', 'handicap', 'crippled', 'blind' and 'deaf' are used synonymously.

- Destiny is seen as the culprit, and disabled people are the victims. The common perception views disability as retribution for past karma (actions) from which there can be no reprieve.

- The very term 'disabled' challenges each of these assumptions. Terms such as 'mentally challenged', 'visually impaired' and 'physically impaired' came to replace the more trite negative terms such as 'retarded', 'crippled' or 'lame'.

- There is a close relationship between disability and poverty. Malnutrition, mothers weakened by frequent childbirth, inadequate immunisation programmes, accidents in overcrowded homes, all contribute to an incidence of disability among poor people that is higher than among people living in easier circumstances.

Approach Adopted for the Disabled in Census 2011

- Information on disability was collected during the Population Enumeration phase of Census 2011 through 'Household Schedule'.

- Questions on disability were asked about all persons in the household.

- Enumerators were instructed to contact the disabled person in the households, besides the respondent, to collect information.

- All types of household, i.e., 'National', 'Institutional' and 'Household', were covered.

- Questions and instructions on disability were finalised after field trial of selected questions, including disability in selected area; extensive deliberation was held with civil society organisations and nodal ministry; pre-test of all census questions covering rural/urban sample in all States was conducted.

- Aspects considered in finalising questions: simple nomenclature of the types/ categories of disability for easy comprehension by both enumerator and respondent, relevance of data for the planners and policy-makers, feasibility of canvassing the question to cover all types of disabilities as listed in the Persons with Disabilities Act, 1995, and the National Trust Act, 1999.

- A filter question to ascertain disability status was included.

- Attempt was made to collect information on eight types of disabilities as against five in Census 2001.

- The placement of the question on disability in the census Schedule was changed and the question was brought forward.

- Special efforts were made to improve the coverage, which included extensive training to the enumerators and publicity measures.

Exercise

1. Social resources include which of the following types of capital?

   I.   Material assets and income

   II. Educational qualifications

   III. Social associations

   (a) I and II

   (b) II and III

   (c) I and III

   (d) All of the above

2. In Sociology, the term social stratification refers to -

   (a) Division of society on the basis of castes

   (b) Division of society on the basis of economic status

   (c) Ranking of people in a hierarchy

   (d) Varna order division

3. The marriage usually restricted to members of the same caste is of following type?

   (a) Exogamy

   (b) Endogamy

   (c) Heterogeneous

   (d) Homogeneous

4. **Assertion (A):** Prejudices refer to pre-conceived opinions or attitudes held by members of one group towards another.

   Reason (R): A prejudiced person preconceives views oftenly based on hearsay rather than on direct evidence.

   (a) Both A and R are true and R is the correct explanation of A

   (b) Both A and R are true but R is not the correct explanation of A

   (c) A is true and R is false

   (d) A is false and R is true

5. Some communities were characterised as 'martial races', some others as effeminate or cowardly, yet others as untrustworthy. Based on the mentioned description, which of the following is correct?

   (a) Prejudice

   (b) Discrimination

   (c) Stereotype

   (d) Social stratification

6. **Assertion (A):** Dalits may build their own temple, or convert to another religion like Buddhism, Christianity or Islam.

   Reason (R): Prolonged experience of discriminatory or insulting behaviour often produces such reaction among Dalits.

   (a) Both A and R are true and R is the correct explanation of A

   (b) Both A and R are true but R is not the correct explanation of A

   (c) A is true and R is false

   (d) A is false and R is true

7. During colonial period, many Indians initiated and participated in the social reforms due to which of the following reasons?

   I.   Humiliation of colonial rule

   II. Exposure to idea of democracy and justice

   III. Urge to introduce modernity in the society

   (a) I and III

   (b) II and III

   (c) I and II

   (d) All of the above

8. In African society, apartheid emerged due which of the following reason?

   (a) Division of society on the basis of hierarchy

   (b) Political control of White European minority

   (c) To ensure employment to White population

   (d) Promotion of slavery

9. The concept of untouchability in Indian society is based upon?

   (a) Discrimination on the basis of occupation

   (b) Social stratification

   (c) Purity-pollution

   (d) Dalits to be boycotted at social place

10. Which of the following are dimensions of untouchability which defines this phenomenon in Indian society?

    I.   Exclusion

    II. Humiliation

    III. Subordination

    IV. Exploitation

    (a) I and II

    (b) I, II and III

    (c) II, III and IV

    (d) All of the above

11. **Assertion (A):** The ex-untouchable communities and their leaders have coined another term, 'Dalit'.

    Reason (R): The term Dalit conveys the sense of an oppressed people.

    (a) Both A and R are true and R is the correct explanation of A

    (b) Both A and R are true but R is not the correct explanation of A

    (c) A is true and R is false

    (d) A is false and R is true

12. Choose the incorrect statement about Dalit Panthers:

    (a) It was a radical group emerged in Western India

    (b) They fought to assert their identity

    (c) They struggled for their rights and dignity

    (d) It is the philosophy of Dr. B. R. Ambedkar to empower the group

13. Which of the following statement is incorrect regarding initiatives taken by state against discrimination?

(a) The listings of schedules to castes and tribes was initiated in Govt. of India Act 1935.

(b) Other Backward classes got their recognition in Indian Independence Act 1947.

(c) Reservation was introduced to compensate past and present discrimination.

(d) Untouchability is prohibited in Constitution after independence.

14. The First Backward Classes Commission was headed by -

(a) Jawaharlal Nehru   (b) Babu Jagjeevan Ram

(c) Kaka Kalelkar   (d) (b) R. Ambedkar

15. Which of the following changes in Adivasis life had taken place after independence of India?

I. Government monopoly over forests continued

II. Adivasis lands had been acquired

III. Rehabilitation centres were made for their protection

(a) I and II   (b) II and III

(c) I and III   (d) All of the above

16. The Independence of India in 1947 should have made life easier for adivasis but this was not the case. This happened due to which of the following reason?

(a) Dam and building construction

(b) Minorities had given rights but not implemented properly

(c) Internal colonialism

(d) No compensation or rehabilitation were given

17. In Indian society, what does the term Adivasi connotes?

(a) Local inhabitants

(b) Original inhabitants

(c) Untouchables

(d) Displaced population

18. 'The Texts of the Hindu Law' was written which of the following personality?

(a) Raja Rammohan Roy

(b) B.R. Ambedkar

(c) M. G. Ranade

(d) Mahatma Gandhi

19. Which of the following text is the earliest example of science fiction writing in India?

(a) Bhagwad Geeta

(b) Stree Purush Tulna

(c) Precepts of Jesus

(d) Sultana's Dream

20. Which of the following factors contribute to an incidence of disability in society?

I. Malnutrition

II. Inadequate immunization

III. Accidents in overcrowded homes

(a) I and II

(b) II and III

(c) II only

(d) All of the above

Answer Keys

1. (d)	**2.** (c)	**3.** (b)	**4.** (a)	**5.** (c)	**6.** (a)	**7.** (c)	**8.** (b)	**9.** (c)	**10.** (d)
11. (a)	**12.** (d)	**13.** (b)	**14.** (c)	**15.** (d)	**16.** (c)	**17.** (b)	**18.** (c)	**19.** (d)	**20.** (d)

CHAPTER 6

Challenges of Cultural Diversity

Chapter at Glance

- The term 'diversity' emphasises differences rather than inequalities. When we say that India is a nation of great cultural diversity, we mean that there are many different types of social groups and communities living here.

- The difficulties arise from the fact that cultural identities are very powerful - they can arouse intense passions and are often able to moblise large numbers of people.

- Sometimes cultural differences are accompanied by economic and social inequalities, and this further complicates things.

The Importance Of Community Identity

- Community identity is based on birth and 'belonging' rather than on some form of acquired qualifications or 'accomplishment'. It is what we 'are' rather than what we have 'become'.

- These kinds of identities are called 'ascriptive' - that is, they are determined by the accidents of birth and do not involve any choice on the part of the individuals concerned.

- A second feature of ascriptive identities and community feeling is that they are universal. Everyone has a motherland, a mother tongue, a family, a faith... This may not necessarily be strictly true of every individual, but it is true in a general sense.

- It is a social fact that no country or group ever mobilises its members to struggle for untruth, injustice or inequality - everyone is always fighting for truth, justice, equality.

Communities, Nations And Nation-States

- In its most general sense, the term state refers to an abstract entity consisting of a set of political-legal institutions claiming control over a particular geographical territory and the people living in it. In Max Weber's well-known definition, a state is a "body that successfully claims a monopoly of legitimate force in a particular territory".

- A nation is a peculiar sort of community that is easy to describe but hard to define.

- We know and can describe many specific nations founded on the basis of common cultural, historical and political institutions like a shared religion, language, ethnicity, history or regional culture.

- But it is hard to come up with any defining features, any characteristics that a nation must possess.

- Today, 'the nation' is the most accepted or proper justification for a state, while 'the people' are the ultimate source of legitimacy of the nation. In other words, states 'need' the nation as much or even more than nations need states.

Assimilationist and integrationist strategies try to establish singular national identities through various interventions like:

- Centralising all power to forums where the dominant group constitutes a majority, and eliminating the autonomy of local or minority groups;

- Imposing a unified legal and judicial system based on the dominant group's traditions and abolishing alternative systems used by other groups;

- Adopting the dominant group's language as the only official 'national' language and making its use mandatory in all public institutions;

- Promotion of the dominant group's language and culture through national institutions including state-controlled media and educational institutions;

- Adoption of state symbols celebrating the dominant group's history, heroes and culture, reflected in such things as choice of national holidays or naming of streets etc.;

- Seizure of lands, forests and fisheries from minority groups and indigenous people and declaring them 'national resources'.

- Policies that promote assimilation are aimed at persuading, encouraging or forcing all citizens to adopt a uniform set of cultural values and norms.

- These values and norms are usually entirely or largely those of the dominant social group. Other, non-dominant or subordinated groups in society are expected or required to give up their own cultural values and adopt the prescribed ones.

- Policies promoting integration are different in style but not in overall objective: they insist that the public culture be restricted to a common national pattern, while all 'non-national' cultures are to be relegated to the private sphere.

- In this case too, there is the danger of the dominant group's culture being treated as 'national' culture.

An Overview On Cultural Diversity And The Indian Nation-State

- The Indian nation-state is socially and culturally one of the most diverse countries of the world.

- It has a population of about 1.21 billion people, according to Census of India 2011, currently the second largest - and soon to become the largest - national population in the world.

- These billion-plus people speak about 1,632 different languages and dialects.

- As many as twenty two of these languages have been officially recognised and placed under the 8th Schedule of the Constitution, thus guaranteeing their legal status.

- In terms of religion, about 80% of the population are Hindus, who in turn are regionally specific, plural in beliefs and practices, and divided by castes and languages.

- About 14.2% of the population are Muslims, which makes India the world's second largest Muslim country after Indonesia and Pakistan.

- The other major religious communities are Christians (2.3%), Sikhs (1.7%), Buddhists (0.7%) and Jains (0.4%). Because of India's huge population, these small percentages can also add up to large absolute numbers.

- In terms of the nation-state's relationship with community identities, the Indian case fits neither the assimilationist nor the integrationist model.

- The Constitution declares the state to be a secular state, but religion, language and other such factors are not banished from the public sphere.

- India can be considered a good example of a 'state-nation' though it is not entirely free from the problems common to nation-states.

Regionalism In The Indian Context

- Regionalism in India is rooted in India's diversity of languages, cultures, tribes, and religions.

- It is also encouraged by the geographical concentration of these identity markers in particular regions, and fuelled by a sense of regional deprivation.

- Indian federalism has been a means of accommodating these regional sentiments.

- After Independence, initially the Indian state continued with the British-Indian arrangement dividing India into large provinces, also called 'presidencies'.

- These were large multi-ethnic and multilingual provincial states constituting the major political-administrative units of a semi-federal state called the Union of India.

- The old Bombay State (continuation of the Bombay Presidency) was a multilingual state of Marathi, Gujarati, Kannada and Konkani speaking people. Similarly, the Madras State was constituted by Tamil, Telugu, Kannada and Malayalam speaking people.

- The larger princely states included Mysore, Kashmir, and Baroda. But soon after the adoption of the Constitution, all these units of the colonial era had to be reorganised into ethno-linguistic States within the Indian union in response to strong popular agitations.

- Language coupled with regional and tribal identity - and not religion - has therefore provided the most powerful instrument for the formation of ethno-national identity in India.

- In the creation of three new states in 2000, namely Chhatisgarh, Uttaranchal and Jharkhand, language did not play a prominent role. Rather, a combination of ethnicity based on tribal identity, language, regional deprivation and ecology provided the basis for intense regionalism resulting in statehood.
- Respecting regional sentiments is not just a matter of creating States: this has to be backed up with an institutional structure that ensures their viability as relatively autonomous units within a larger federal structure.

Constitutional Provisions

- Constitutional provisions defining the powers of the States and the Centre.
- There are lists of 'subjects' or areas of governance which are the exclusive responsibility of either State or Centre, along with a 'Concurrent List' of areas where both are allowed to operate.
- The State legislatures determine the composition of the upper house of Parliament, the Rajya Sabha.
- There are periodic committees and commissions that decide on Centre-State relations.

Some Challenges and Suggested Solution

- Since the era of liberalisation (i.e., since the 1990s) there is concern among policy makers, politicians and scholars about increasing inter-regional economic and infrastructural inequalities.
- As private investment (both foreign and Indian) is given a greater role in economic development, considerations of regional equity get diluted.
- This happens because private investors generally want to invest in already developed States where the infrastructure and other facilities are better.
- Unlike private industry, the government can give some consideration to regional equity (and other social goals) rather than just seek to maximise profits.
- So left to itself, the market economy tends to increase the gap between developed and backward regions. Fresh public initiatives will be needed to reverse current trends.

The Nation-State And Religion-Related Issues And Identities

- Perhaps the most contentious of all aspects of cultural diversity are issues relating to religious communities and religion-based identities. These issues may be broadly divided into two related groups - the secularism-communalism set and the minority-majority set.

Minority Rights And Nation Building

- In Indian nationalism, the dominant trend was marked by an inclusive and democratic vision. Inclusive because it recognised diversity and plurality. Democratic because it sought to do away with discrimination and exclusion and bring forth a just and equitable society.
- The notion of minority groups is widely used in sociology and is more than a merely numerical distinction - it usually involves some sense of relative disadvantage.
- Thus, privileged minorities such as extremely wealthy people are not usually referred to as minorities; if they are, the term is qualified in some way, as in the phrase 'privileged minority'.
- When minority is used without qualification, it generally implies a relatively small but also disadvantaged group.
- The sociological sense of minority also implies that the members of the minority form a collectivity - that is, they have a strong sense of group solidarity, a feeling of togetherness and belonging.
- This is linked to disadvantage because the experience of being subjected to prejudice and discrimination usually heightens feelings of intra-group loyalty and interests.
- Religious or cultural minorities need special protection because of the demographic dominance of the majority. In democratic politics, it is always possible to convert a numerical majority into political power through elections.
- This means that religious or cultural minorities - regardless of their economic or social position - are politically vulnerable.

Constitutional Provisions

- The makers of the Indian Constitution were aware that a strong and united nation could be built only when all sections of people had the freedom to practice their religion, and to develop their culture and language.
- Dr. B.R. Ambedkar, the chief architect of the Constitution, made this point clear in the Constituent Assembly.

Article 29:

(1) Any section of the citizens residing in the territory of India or any part thereof having a distinct language, script or culture of its own shall have the right to conserve the same.

(2) No citizen shall be denied admission into any educational institution maintained by the State or received out of State funds on grounds only of religion, race, caste, language or any of them.

Article 30:

(1) All minorities, whether based on religion or language, shall have the right to establish and administer educational institutions of their choice.

(2) The State shall not, in granting aid to educational institutions, discriminate against any educational institution on the ground that it is under the management of a minority, whether based on religion or language.

Communalism, Secularism And The Nation-State

Communalism

- 'Communalism' refers to aggressive chauvinism based on religious identity.

- Communalism is an aggressive political ideology linked to religion.

- It is important to emphasise that communalism is about politics, not about religion. Although communalists are intensely involved with religion, there is in fact no necessary relationship between personal faith and communalism.

- A communalist may or may not be a devout person, and devout believers may or may not be communalists. However, all communalists do believe in a political identity based on religion.

- One of the characteristic features of communalism is its claim that religious identity overrides everything else. Whether one is poor or rich, whatever one's occupation, caste or political beliefs, it is religion alone that counts.

- India has had a history of communal riots from pre-Independence times, often as a result of the divide-and-rule policy adopted by the colonial rulers.

- But colonialism did not invent inter-community conflicts - there is also a long history of pre-colonial conflicts - and it certainly cannot be blamed for post-Independence riots and killings.

Secularism

- The word secularism is among the most complex terms in social and political theory.

- In the western context the main sense of these terms has to do with the separation of church and state. The separation of religious and political authority marked a major turning point in the social history of the west.

- The Indian meanings of secular and secularism include the western sense but also involve others. The most common use of secular in everyday language is as the opposite of communal. So, a secular person or state is one that does not favour any particular religion over others.

- The first generation of leaders of independent India (who happened to be overwhelmingly Hindu and upper caste) chose to have a liberal, secular state governed by a democratic constitution.

- Accordingly, the 'state' was conceived in culturally neutral terms, and the 'nation' was also conceived as an inclusive territorial-political community of all citizens. Nation building was viewed mainly as a state-driven process of economic development and social transformation.

State And Civil Society

- The state is indeed a very crucial institution when it comes to the management of cultural diversity in a nation.

- To the extent that the state structure - the legislature, bureaucracy, judiciary, armed forces, police and other arms of the state - becomes insulated from the people, it also has the potential of turning authoritarian.

- Authoritarian states often limit or abolish civil liberties like freedom of speech, freedom of the press, freedom of political activity, right to protection from wrongful use of authority, right to the due processes of the law, and so on.

- Apart from authoritarianism, there is also the possibility that state institutions become unable or unwilling to respond to the needs of the people because of corruption, inefficiency, or lack of resources.

- Non-state actors and institutions become important in this context, for they can keep a watch on the state, protest against its injustices or supplement its efforts.

Civil Society

- Civil society is the non-state and non-market part of the public domain in which individuals get together voluntarily to create institutions and organisations.

- It is the sphere of active citizenship: here, individuals take up social issues, try to influence the state or make demands on it, pursue their collective interests or seek support for a variety of causes.

- It consists of voluntary associations, organisations or institutions formed by groups of citizens.

- It includes political parties, media institutions, trade unions, non-governmental organisations (NGOs), religious organisations, and other kinds of collective entities.

- The main criteria for inclusion in civil society are that the organisation should not be state-controlled, and it should not be a purely commercial profit-making entity.

- Among the most significant recent initiatives is the campaign for the Right to Information. Beginning with an agitation in rural Rajasthan for the release of information on government funds spent on village development, this effort grew into a nation-wide campaign.

Forcing the State to Respond to the People: The Right to Information Act

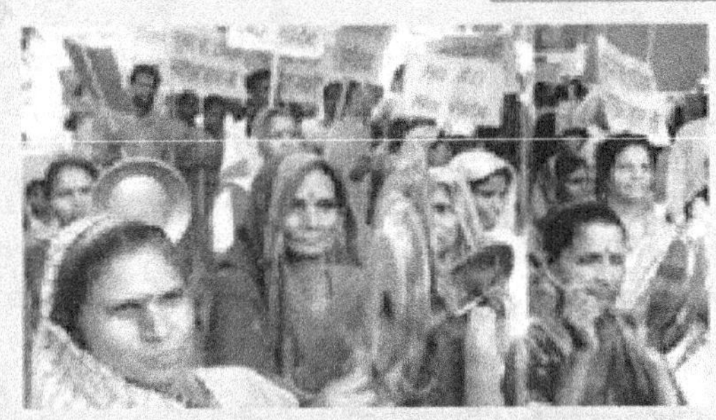

The Right to Information Act 2005 (Act No. 22/ 2005) is a law enacted by the Parliament of India giving Indians access to Government records. Under the terms of the Act, any person may request information from a "public authority" (a body of Government or instrumentality of State) which is expected to reply expeditiously or within thirty days. The Act also requires every public authority to computerise their records for wide dissemination and to proactively publish certain categories of information so that the citizens need minimum recourse to request for information formally.

This law was passed by Parliament on 15 June 2005 and came into force on 13 October 2005. Information disclosure in India was hitherto restricted by the Official Secrets Act 1923 and various other special laws, which the new RTI Act now overrides.

The Act specifies that citizens have a right to:

> request any information (as defined)

> take copies of documents

> inspect documents, works and records

> take certified samples of materials of work.

> obtain information in the form of printouts, diskettes, floppies, tapes, video cassettes or in any other electronic mode.

Exercise

1. In sociology, the births determined by accident and do not involve any choice on the part of the individuals concerned. This identity is known as -

   (a) Ascriptive identity   (b) Descriptive identity

   (c) Varna system   (d) Social structure

2. **Assertion (A):** People often react emotionally or even violently whenever there is a perceived threat to their community identity.

   Reason (R): Expanding and overlapping circles of community ties like family, kinship, caste, ethnicity, language, region or religion, etc. give meaning to our world and give us a sense of identity, of who we are.

   (a) Both A and R are true and R is the correct explanation of A.

   (b) Both A and R are true but R is not the correct explanation of A.

   (c) A is true and R is false.

   (d) A is false and R is true.

3. Which of following are features of ascriptive identity in society?

   I. Sense of brotherhood

   II. Sense of belongingness

   III. Universal in nature

   (a) I and II

   (b) II and III

   (c) I and III

   (d) All of the above

4. A nation can be described on the following basis -

   I. Culture

   II. History

   III. Political institutions

   (a) I and II

   (b) II and III

   (c) I and III

   (d) All of the above

5. Which of the following are geographical distant territories of the same nation?

   (a) Austria and Germany

   (b) Saudi Arabia and United Arab Emirates

   (c) Falkland and United Kingdom

   (d) Venezuela and Ecuador

6. Which of the following policies promote assimilation in the society?

   I. Persuasion

   II. Encourage

   III. Forceful adoption of culture

   (a) I and III

   (b) I and II

   (c) II and III

   (d) All of the above

7. Choose the incorrect statement about cultural diversity.

   (a) 22 languages are officially recognized under Constitution which guarantees legal status to it.

   (b) India is world's second largest Muslim country after Pakistan.

   (c) More than 1000 different languages and dialects are spoken by Indian population.

   (d) Hindu population in India and plural in beliefs and practices.

8. In terms of the nation-state's relationship with community identities India's case fits into -

   (a) Assimilationist

   (b) Integrationist

   (c) Mixture of assimilation and integration

   (d) Neither assimilationist not integrationist

9. The idea of division of states on linguistic basis was supported by India during -

   (a) Govt. of India Act 1919

   (b) Congress session of 1920

   (c) Govt. of India Act 1935

   (d) Indian Independence Act 1947

10. The most powerful instrument for the formation of ethno- national identity in India is -

    I. Language

    II. Religion

    III. Region identity

    IV. Tribal identity

    (a) I, II and III

    (b) II, III and IV

    (c) I, III and IV

    (d) All of the above

11. The creation of three new states in 2000, namely Chhatisgarh, Uttaranchal and Jharkhand has happened on the following basis:

(a) Language

(b) Religion

(c) Tribal identity

(d) Tourism

12. The Centre-State relationship is determined by which of the following ways?

I. Periodic committees

II. Division of subjects

III. Composition of Rajya Sabha

(a) I and II

(b) II and III

(c) I and III

(d) All of the above

Read the following passage and answer the questions 13, 14 and 15.

On the whole the federal system has worked fairly well, though there remain many contentious issues. Since the era of liberalisation (i.e., since the 1990s) there is concern among policy makers, politicians and scholars about increasing inter-regional economic and infrastructural inequalities. As private investment (both foreign and Indian) is given a greater role in economic development, considerations of regional equity get diluted. This happens because private investors generally want to invest in already developed States where the infrastructure and other facilities are better. Unlike private industry, the government can give some consideration to regional equity (and other social goals) rather than just seek to maximise profits. So left to itself, the market economy tends to increase the gap between developed and backward regions. Fresh public initiatives will be needed to reverse current trends.

13. Which of the following statement is incorrect about regionalism?

(a) The regional equity is promoted due to private investments after liberalization.

(b) Investment and infrastructure development by private investors in developed states majorly.

(c) Private investors have taken keen interest in economic development.

(d) Market economy tend to increase the gap between developed and deprived states.

14. Regional equity is hampered due to -

(a) Ignorance of government's consideration in regional development.

(b) Profit making motto of private investors

(c) Cultural identity is ignored due to infrastructure development

(d) Displacement of tribal population.

15. The current trends of market has increased the gap between developed and backward regions. It can be overcome through -

(a) More foreign investment

(b) Infrastructure development

(c) More public investment

(d) Financial investment for economic growth

16. In sociological sense, the term minority is defined as -

(a) Individually have a strong sense of group solidarity, a feeling of togetherness and belonging.

(b) Less number of population in a particular region.

(c) Tribal community who had been deprived of basic rights.

(d) A group of population who collectively have a strong sense of group solidarity, a feeling of togetherness and belonging.

17. The religious minorities like the Parsis or Sikhs may be relatively well-off economically, however, they are disadvantaged due to following reason:

(a) In cultural sense they are small in number

(b) Due to secular state, India do not promote their culture and religion

(c) Lack of their assimilation in society

(d) They are major group in particular region

18. National unity in India weakens due to which of the following reason?

(a) Conversion of religion on the basis of persuasion.

(b) Forcible imposition of language and religion

(c) Terrorist activities on the borders

(d) Rise of rational new generation in society

19. The limiting or abolishing civil liberties like freedom of speech, freedom of the press, freedom of political activity, right to protection from wrongful use of authority, right to the due processes of the law, etc. is feature of which of state type?

(a) Monarchy

(b) Democratic state

(c) Communist state

(d) Authoritarian state

20. Which of the following statements are correct regarding civil society?

I. Individuals may voluntarily create institutions and organizations

II. Individuals may take up social issues and influence the state

III. Organization formed will be state-controlled.

(a) I and II   (b) II and III

(c) I and III   (d) All of the above

Answer Keys

1. (a)	**2.** (a)	**3.** (b)	**4.** (d)	**5.** (c)	**6.** (d)	**7.** (b)	**8.** (d)	**9.** (b)	**10.** (c)
11. (c)	**12.** (d)	**13.** (a)	**14.** (b)	**15.** (c)	**16.** (d)	**17.** (a)	**18.** (b)	**19.** (d)	**20.** (a)

PART – II

Structural Changes

Chapter at Glance

- English is not only widely used in India but we now have an impressive body of literary writings by Indians in English.
- Colonialism brought into being new political, economic and social structural changes.
- All these structural changes were accompanied by cultural changes.

Understanding Colonialism

- Colonialism simply means the establishment of rule by one country over another. In the modern period western colonialism has had the greatest impact.
- The impact of colonial rule is distinguishable from all other earlier rules because the changes it brought in were far-reaching and deep.
- Nevertheless, there is a vital difference between the empire building of pre-capitalist times and that of capitalist times.
- The pre-capitalist conquerors benefited from their domination by exacting a continuous flow of tribute.
- British colonialism which was based on a capitalist system directly interfered to ensure greatest profit and benefit to British capitalism.
- It changed not just land ownership laws but decided even what crops ought to be grown and what ought not to be.
- It altered the way production and distribution of goods took place. It entered into the forests. It cleared trees and started tea plantations.
- It brought in Forest Acts that changed the lives of pastoralists.
- Colonialism also led to considerable movement of people. It led to movement of people from one part to another within India.
- For instance people from present day Jharkhand moved to Assam to work on the tea plantations.

- A newly emerging middle class particularly from the British Presidency regions of Bengal and Madras moved as government employees and professionals like doctors and lawyers moved to different parts of the country.
- People were carted in ships from India to work on other colonised lands in distant Asia, Africa and Americas.
- Many died on their way. Most could never return. Today many of their descendents are known as people of Indian origin.

Depth of Structural Changes

- This magnitude and depth of the structural changes that colonialism unleashed can be better grasped if we try and understand some basic features of capitalism.
- Capitalism is an economic system in which the means of production are privately owned and organised to accumulate profits within a market system.
- Capitalism in the west emerged out of a complex process of European exploration of the rest of the world, its plunder of wealth and resources, an unprecedented growth of science and technology, its harnessing to industries and agriculture.
- Western colonialism was inextricably connected to the growth of western capitalism.
- If capitalism became the dominant economic system, nation states became the dominant political form.
- Nationalism implied that the people of India or of any colonised society have an equal right to be sovereign.
- Indian nationalist leaders were quick to grasp this irony. They declared that freedom or swaraj was their birth-right and fought for both political and economic freedom.

Urbanisation And Industrialisation

- Industrialisation refers to the emergence of machine production, based on the use of inanimate power resources like steam or electricity.

- The relatively low level of technological development did not permit more than a small minority to be freed from the chores of agricultural production.

- In India the impact of the very same British industrialisation led to deindustrialisation in some sectors.

- Just as manufacturing boomed in Britain, traditional exports of cotton and silk manufactures from India declined in the face of Manchester competition.

- This period also saw the further decline of cities such as Surat and Masulipatnam while Bombay and Madras grew.

- When the British took over Indian states, towns like Thanjavur, Dhaka, and Murshidabad lost their courts and, therefore, some of their artisans and court gentry.

- From the end of the 19th century, with the installation of mechanised factory industries, some towns became much more heavily populated.

- Unlike Britain where the impact of industrialisation led to more people moving into urban areas, in India the initial impact of the same British industrialisation led to more people moving into agriculture. The Census of India Report shows this clearly.

Development of Cities

- Cities had a key role in the economic system of empires. Coastal cities such as Mumbai, Kolkata and Chennai were favoured.

- From here primary commodities could be easily exported and manufactured goods could be cheaply imported.

- Colonial cities were the prime link between the economic centre or core in Britain and periphery or margins in colonised India.

- Cities in this sense were the concrete expression of global capitalism.

- In British India for example Bombay was planned and re-developed so that by 1900 over three-quarters of India's raw cotton were shipped through the city.

- Calcutta exported jute to Dundee while Madras sent coffee, sugar, indigo dyes and cotton to Britain.

- Urbanisation in the colonial period saw the decline of some earlier urban centres and the emergence of new colonial cities.

- Kolkata was one of the first of such cities. In 1690, an English merchant named Job Charnock arranged to lease three villages (named Kolikata, Gobindapur, and Sutanuti) by the river Hugli in order to set up a trading post.

- In 1698, Fort William was established by the river for defensive purposes, and a large open area was cleared around the fort for military engagements. The fort and the open area (called Maidan) formed the core of the city that emerged rather rapidly.

Industrialisation In Independent India

- For Indian nationalists the issue of economic exploitation under colonial rule was a central issue.

- Images of pre-colonial fabled riches of India contrasted with the poverty of British India.

- The Swadeshi movement strengthened the loyalty to the national economy.

- Indian nationalists saw rapid industrialisation of the economy as the path towards both growth and social equity.

- Development of heavy and machine-making industries, expansion of the public sector and holding of a large cooperative sector were considered very important.

Urbanisation In Independent India

- Writing on the different kinds of urbanisation witnesses in the first two decades after independence sociologist M.S.A. Rao argued that in India many villages all over India are becoming increasingly subject to the impact of urban influences.

- But the nature of urban impact varies according to the kind of relations a village has with a city or town. He describes three different situations of urban impact:

  - Firstly, there are villages in which a sizeable number of people have sought employment in far-off cities. They live there leaving behind the members of their families in their natal villages.

  - The second kind of urban impact is to be seen in villages which are situated near an industrial town. When an industrial town like Bhilai comes up in the midst of villages, some villages are totally uprooted while the lands of others are partially acquired.

- The growth of metropolitan cities accounts for the third type of urban impact on the surrounding villages. While a few villages are totally absorbed in the process of expansion, only the land of many others, excluding the inhabited area, is used for urban development.

Rise in Urban Population

- In 1951, 17.29% of India's population i.e., 62.44 million people, were living in 2,843 towns. In 2011, 31.16% of India's population i.e., 377.10 million people, were living in 7,935 towns.

- This shows a steady increase in terms of absolute numbers, number of UA/towns and the per cent share of the urban population.

- However, the decennial growth rate of the urban population showed a declining trend during 1981-2001, reversed the trend and showed marginal increase in 2011.

- The decennial growth rate of the urban population in 1951 was 41.42% and in 2011, it was 31.80%.

- For the first time since Independence, the absolute increase in population is more in urban areas than in rural areas.

- This is due to a sharp decline in the growth rate in rural areas, while the growth rate in urban areas remains almost the same.

Exercise

1. Which of the following are introduced in India due to colonialism?

    I.   Street food

    II. Education and law system

    III. Eateries like biscuits

    (a) I and II   (b) I and III

    (c) II and III   (d) All of the above

2. Choose the incorrect statement regarding pre-capitalist period:

    (a) Conquerors benefitted from their domination by collecting tributes.

    (b) Their interference in economic base can be marked as ruin of handicraft in India.

    (c) They used to collect tribute from the economic surplus.

    (d) Annexation of territories was a common feature.

3. Which of the following is correct about western education in India?

    (a) It was introduced to spread western thoughts like democracy and equality.

    (b) It was introduced to make Indian society modernized.

    (c) It was introduced to create a momentum of nationalism.

    (d) It was introduced to create Indians who could manage British colonialism.

4. Which of the following cities declined due to manufacturing boom in Britain?

    I.   Surat

    II. Bombay

    III. Masulipatnam

    (a) I and II

    (b) II only

    (c) I and III

    (d) All of the above

Read the following passage and answer question nos. 5 and 6

Urban luxury manufactures like the high quality silks and cottons of Dacca or Murshidabad must have been hit first by the almost simultaneous collapse of indigeneous court demand and the external market on which these had largely depended. Village crafts in the interior, and particularly, in regions other than eastern India where British penetration was earliest and deepest, probably survived much longer, coming to be seriously affected only with the spread of railways.

5. Indigeneous industries of textiles collapsed due to which of the following reason?

    (a) Fall in the court demand

    (b) Decline in the external market demand

    (c) Both (a) and (b)

    (d) Neither (a) nor (b)

6. Choose the incorrect statement:

(a) Railways led to the decline in indigenous village crafts.

(b) Machine made cotton clothes were more comfortable than the Indian made.

(c) Machine made textiles were more in demand as compared to Indian handmade clothes.

(d) Murshidabad was the main and prosperous textile manufacturing center during pre-colonial time.

7. Which of the statement is correct about Industrialization in India by Britain?

(a) It led more people move into urban areas.

(b) It led to more people moved into agriculture.

(c) It led to the emergence of new educated class in India.

(d) It led to the conversion of agricultural economy into industrial economy

8. Cities had a key role in the economic system of empires. How?

(a) It provide easy import and export of commodities

(b) It provide a link between core centre and periphery centres in the colonies.

(c) Both (a) and (b)

(d) Neither (a) nor (b)

9. **Assertion (A):** Capitalism in the west emerged out of a complex process of European exploration of the rest of the world, its plunder of wealth and resources.

Reason (R): Western colonialism was inextricably connected to the growth of western capitalism.

(a) Both A and R are true and R is the correct reason of A.

(b) Both A and R are true and R is not the correct reason of A.

(c) A is true and R is false.

(d) A is false and R is true.

10. In 1690, an English merchant named Job Charnock arranged to lease which of the following villages?

I. Sutanuti

II. Chandannagore

III. Kalikata

(a) I and II   (b) II and III

(c) I and III   (d) All of the above

11. Which of the following commodities were sent by Madras to Britain in 20th C?

I. Jute   II. Sugar

III. Indigo   IV. Cotton

(a) I, II and III   (b) II, III and IV

(c) III and IV   (d) All of the above

12. The sociologist M.S.A. Rao argued that in India many villages all over India are becoming increasingly subject to the impact of urban influences. Choose the correct statement regarding this:

I. Villages having sizeable population seek employment in far-off cities.

II. Villages which are situated near an industrial town.

III. Growth of metropolitan cities.

(a) I and II

(b) III

(c) II and III

(d) All of the above

13. **Assertion (A):** For the first time since Independence, the absolute increase in population is more in urban areas than in rural areas.

Reason (R): A sharp decline in the growth rate in rural areas, while the growth rate in urban areas remains almost the same.

(a) Both A and R are true and R is the correct reason of A.

(b) Both A and R are true and R is not the correct reason of A.

(c) A is true and R is false.

(d) A is false and R is true.

14. Prior to independence, who was the Chairman of National Planning Committee?

(a) K. T. Shah

(b) Jawaharlal Nehru

(c) Abul Kalam Azad

(d) Sardar Vallabhbhai Patel

15. Industrialisation and urbanisation did not happen in India quite the way it did in Britain. The reason of this was -

(a) Late beginning of industrialization in India

(b) Fragmentation of Indian polity

(c) Early industrialisation and urbanisation were governed by colonial interests

(d) Lack of economic unification

16. The capitalist system of British Rule started interfering into -

I. Manufacturing sector

II. Law of the land

III. Crops to be cultivated

(a) I and II

(b) II and III

(c) I and III

(d) All of the above

17. Lives of pastoralists got affected under British Rule -

    (a) Forest law

    (b) Conversion of religion

    (c) Interfere in the lives of forest dwellers

    (d) Rule of animal husbandry

18. Choose the incorrect statement:

    (a) Colonialism also led to considerable movement of people.

    (b) People from Jharkhand moved to Assam to work on the tea plantations.

    (c) A newly emerging middle class from the British Presidency regions of Bengal, Bombay and Madras moved as government employees and professionals like doctors and lawyers .

    (d) People were forcefully carted in the ships to colonies of Asia, Africa and Americas.

19. The economic system in which means of production is privately owned and organized to accumulate profits within a market is known as -

    (a) Socialist

    (b) Capitalist

    (c) Mixed economic system

    (d) None of the above

20. Choose the incorrect statement:

    (a) Passport for international travel was started before First World War.

    (b) Nation state pertains to a particular type of state, characteristic of the modern world.

    (c) A government has sovereign power within a defined territorial area, and the people are citizens of a single nation.

    (d) Nation states are closely associated with the rise of nationalism.

Answer Keys

1. (d)	2. (b)	3. (d)	4. (c)	5. (c)	6. (b)	7. (b)	8. (c)	9. (b)	10. (c)
11. (b)	12. (d)	13. (a)	14. (b)	15. (c)	16. (d)	17. (a)	18. (c)	19. (b)	20. (a)

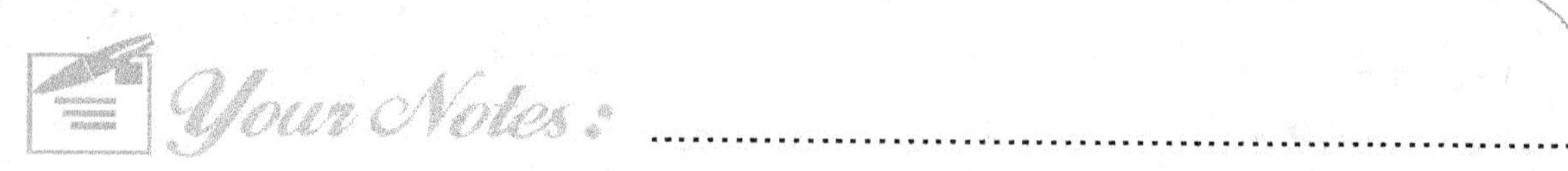

Your Notes : ....

CHAPTER 2

Cultural Change

Chapter at Glance

Social Reform Movements In The 19th And Early 20th Century

- The social reform movements which emerged in India in the 19th century arose to the challenges that colonial Indian society faced.
- The well-known issues are that of sati, child marriage, ban on widow remarriage and caste discrimination.
- The attempts to fight social discrimination in pre-colonial India were central to Buddhism, to Bhakti and Sufi movements.
- It was a creative combination of modern ideas of western liberalism and a new look on traditional literature.

Ideas of Reformers

- Raja Ram Mohun Roy attacked the practice of sati on the basis of both appeals to humanitarian and natural rights doctrines as well as Hindu shastras.
- Ranade's writings entitled The Texts of the Hindu Law on the Lawfulness of the Remarriage of Widows and Vedic Authorities for Widow Marriage elaborated the shastric sanction for remarriage of widows.
- The content of new education was modernising and liberal. The literary content of the courses in the humanities and social sciences was drawn from the literature of the European Renaissance, Reformation and Enlightenment. Its themes were humanistic, secular and liberal.
- Sir Sayed Ahmed Khan's interpretation of Islam emphasised the validity of free enquiry (ijtihad) and the alleged similarities between Koranic revelations and the laws of nature discovered by modern science.
- Kandukiri Viresalingam's The Sources of Knowledge reflected his familiarity with navya-nyaya logic. At the same time he translated the works of Julius Huxley, an eminent biologist.

Sociologist Satish Saberwal elaborates upon the modern context through modern framework of change in colonial India:

- Modes of communication
- Forms of organisation, and
- The nature of ideas

Role of Communication

- New technologies speeded up various forms of communication.
- The printing press, telegraph, and later the microphone, movement of people and goods through steamship and railways helped quick movement of new ideas.
- Within India, social reformers from Punjab and Bengal exchanged ideas with reformers from Madras and Maharashtra. Keshav Chandra Sen of Bengal visited Madras in 1864.
- Pandita Ramabai travelled to different corners of the country. Some of them went to other countries.
- Christian missionaries reached remote corners of present day Nagaland, Mizoram and Meghalaya.
- Modern social organisations like the Brahmo Samaj in Bengal and Arya Samaj in Punjab were set up.
- The All-India Muslim Ladies Conference (Anjuman-E-Khawatn-E-Islam) was founded in 1914.
- Indian reformers debated not just in public meetings but through public media like newspapers and journals.
- Translations of writings of social reformers from one Indian language to another took place.
- For instance, Vishnu Shastri published a Marathi translation of Vidyasagar's book in Indu Prakash in 1868.
- New ideas of liberalism and freedom, new ideas of homemaking and marriage, new roles for mothers and daughters, new ideas of self-conscious pride in culture and tradition emerged.

- The idea of female education was debated intensely. Significantly, it was the social reformer Jotiba Phule who opened the first school for women in Pune.

- Jotiba Phule thus recalled the glory of preAryan age while others like Bal Gangadhar Tilak emphasised the glory of the Aryan period.

Opposing the Reforms

- The varied social reform movements did have common themes. Yet there were also significant differences.

- For some the concerns were confined to the problems that the upper caste, middle class women and men faced.

- For others the injustices suffered by the discriminated castes were central questions.

- For some social evils had emerged because of a decline of the true spirit of Hinduism.

- For others caste and gender oppression was intrinsic to the religion. Likewise Muslim social reformers actively debated the meaning of polygamy and purdah. For example, a resolution against the evils of polygamy was proposed by Jahanara Shah Nawas at the All India Muslim Ladies Conference.

- The resolution condemning polygamy caused considerable debate in the Muslim press. Tahsib-e-Niswan, the leading journal for women in the Punjab, came out in favour of the resolve, but others disapproved.

- Sati was opposed by the Brahmo Samaj. Orthodox members of the Hindu community in Bengal formed an organisation called Dharma Sabha and petitioned the British arguing that reformers had no right to interpret sacred texts. Yet another view increasingly voiced by Dalits was a complete rejection of the Hindu fold.

Different Kinds Of Social Change

- The term sanskritisation was coined by M.N. Srinivas. It may be briefly defined as the process by which a 'low' caste or tribe or other group takes over the customs, ritual, beliefs, ideology and style of life of a high and, in particular, a 'twice-born (dwija) caste'.

- The impact of Sanskritisation is many-sided. Its influence can be seen in language, literature, ideology, music, dance, drama, style of life and ritual.

- It is primarily a process that takes place within the Hindu space though Srinivas argued that it was visible even in sects and religious groups outside Hinduism. Studies of different areas, however, show that it operated differently in different parts of the country.

- In those areas where a highly Sanskritised caste was dominant, the culture of the entire region underwent a certain amount of Sanskritisation.

- In regions where the non-Sanskritic castes were dominant, it was their influence that was stronger. This can be termed the process of 'de-Sanskritisation'.

- Sanskritisation suggests a process whereby people want to improve their status through adoption of names and customs of culturally high-placed groups.

Sanskritisation as a Concept has been Criticised at Different Levels:

- It has been criticised for exaggerating social mobility or the scope of 'lower castes' to move up the social ladder

- It has been pointed out that the ideology of sanskritisation accepts the ways of the 'upper caste' as superior and that of the 'lower caste' as inferior. Therefore, the desire to imitate the 'upper caste' is seen as natural and desirable.

- 'Sanskritisation' seems to justify a model that rests on inequality and exclusion. It appears to suggest that to believe in pollution and purity of groups of people is justifiable or all right.

- Since sanskritisation results in the adoption of upper caste rites and rituals it leads to practices of secluding girls and women, adopting dowry practices instead of bride-price and practising caste discrimination against other groups, etc.

- The effect of such a trend is that the key characteristics of dalit culture and society are eroded. For example the very worth of labour which 'lower castes' do is degraded and rendered 'shameful'.

Westernization

- M.N. Srinivas defines westernisation as "the changes brought about in Indian society and culture as a result of over 150 years of British rule, the term subsuming changes occurring at different levels... technology, institutions, ideology and values".

Different kinds of Westernization

- One kind refers to the emergence of a westernised sub-cultural pattern through a minority section of Indians who first came in contact with Western culture.

- This included the sub culture of Indian intellectuals who not only adopted many cognitive patterns, or ways of thinking, and styles of life, but supported its expansion.

- Westernisation does involve the imitation of external forms of culture. It does not necessarily mean that people adopt modern values of democracy and equality.
- There were, therefore, small sections of people who adopted western life styles or were affected by western ways of thinking.
- Apart from this there has been also the general spread of Western cultural traits, such as the use of new technology, dress, food, and changes in the habits and styles of people in general.

Influence of Westernization

- Apart from ways of life and thinking the west influenced Indian art and literature.
- Artists like Ravi Varma, Abanindranath Tagore, Chandu Menon and Bankimchandra Chattopadhya were all grappling with the colonial encounter.
- The style, technique and the very theme of Ravi Varma were shaped by western and indigeneous traditions.
- It discusses the portrait of a family in a matrilineal community of Kerala but one that significantly resembles the very typical patrilineal nuclear family of the modern west consisting of the father, mother and children.
- In the contemporary context often conflicts between generations are seen as cultural conflicts resulting from westernization.
- Srinivas suggested that while 'lower castes' sought to be Sanskritised, 'upper castes' sought to be Westernised.

Modernisation And Secularisation

- The term modernisation has a long history. From the 19th and more so the 20th century the term began to be associated with positive and desirable values.
- In the early years, modernisation referred to improvement in technology and production processes.
- It referred to the path of development that much of west Europe or North America has taken. And suggested that other societies both have to and ought to follow the same path of development.
- The story of our modernisation and secularisation is, therefore, quite distinct from their growth in the west.
- In the modern west, secularisation has usually meant a process of decline in the influence of religion.
- It has been an assumption of all theorists of modernisation that modern societies become increasingly secular.
- Indicators of secularisation have referred to levels of involvement with religious organisations (such as rates of church attendance), the social and material influence of religious organisations, and the degree to which people hold religious beliefs.
- Recent years have seen an unprecedented growth of religious consciousness and conflict world over.

Exercise

1. **Assertion (A):** The social reform movements which emerged in India in the 19th century arose to the challenges that colonial Indian society faced.

   Reason (R): It was a creative combination of modern ideas of western liberalism and a new look on traditional literature.

   (a) Both A and R are true and R is the correct explanation of A
   (b) Both A and R are true and R is not the correct explanation of A.
   (c) A is true and R is false
   (d) A is false and R is true

2. The text 'The Texts of the Hindu Law on the Lawfulness of the Remarriage of Widows and Vedic Authorities for Widow Marriage' was written by which of following personality?

   (a) M G Ranade
   (b) Mahatma Gandhi
   (c) Raja Rammohun Roy
   (d) Pandita Ramabai

3. New technologies speeded up various forms of communication. Through which of the following ways quick movement of new ideas took place during colonial period?

   I.   Railways   II. Telegraphs
   III. Bullock carts   IV. Press

   (a) I, II and III   (b) II, III and IV
   (c) I, II and IV   (d) All of the above

4. Anjuman-E-Khawatn-E-Islam was an organization of -
   (a) All India Muslim league
   (b) Regional organization in Punjab
   (c) Patriotic song
   (d) All India Muslim Ladies Conference

5. Who among the following published 'Indu Prakash' in Marathi?
   (a) Ishwarchand Vidyasagar
   (b) Vishnu Shashtri
   (c) Jyotiba Phule
   (d) M G Ranade

6. The first school for women in Pune was opened by -
   (a) Jyotiba Phule   (b) Savitribai Phule
   (c) M G Ranade   (d) Vishnu Shashtri

7. Choose the incorrect statement regarding contribution of leader towards education:
   (a) Jyotiba Phule recalled the glory of pre-Aryan age while B G Tilak emphasized on the glory of Aryan Age.
   (b) Female education was justified on the lines of traditional ideas.
   (c) Female education was important for social progress.
   (d) Female education were made by recourse to both modern and traditional ideas.

8. Banning of Sati practice was opposed by which of the following organization?
   (a) Brahmo Samaj
   (b) Tahsib-e-Niswan
   (c) Dharam Sabha
   (d) Anjuman-E-Khawatn-E-Islam

9. **Assertion (A):** Educated middle class read the thinkers of western enlightenment, philosophers of liberal democracy and dreamt of ushering in a liberal and progressive India.

   Reason (R): Colonialism led to the growth of an English educated Indian middle class.
   (a) Both A and R are true and R is the correct explanation of A.
   (b) Both A and R are true and R is not the correct explanation of A.
   (c) A is true and R is false
   (d) A is false and R is true

10. **Assertion (A):** Sanskritization refers to a process that pertains to social mobility that existed before the onset of colonialism.

    Reason (R): As a 'low' caste or tribe or other group takes over the customs, ritual, beliefs, ideology and style of life of a high and, in particular, a 'twice-born (dwija) caste'.
    (a) Both A and R are true and R is the correct explanation of A.
    (b) Both A and R are true and R is not the correct explanation of A.
    (c) A is true and R is false
    (d) A is false and R is true

Read the following passage and answer the following question from 11 to 13.

Kumud Pawade in her autobiography recounts how a Dalit woman became a Sanskrit teacher. As a student she is drawn towards the study of Sanskrit, perhaps because it is the means through which she can break into a field that was not possible for her to enter on grounds of gender and caste. Perhaps she was drawn towards it because it would enable her to read in the original what the texts have to say about women and the Dalits. As she proceeds with her studies, she meets with varied reactions ranging from surprise to hostility, from guarded acceptance to brutal rejection.

11. What information is reflecting through this passage about the society?
    (a) Division of society
    (b) Atrocities of upper castes on dalits
    (c) Sanskrit dominance on society
    (d) Hostile situation towards dalits

12. Kumud Pawade became Sanskrit teacher. Why this is considered as an achievement?
    (a) She competed and succeeded against the upper caste women
    (b) It will give her the real information mentioned in the original texts about the women
    (c) She was rejected to be part of the Indian society
    (d) Dalit had no rights to become teachers

13. The centre message of this passage is -
    (a) Importance of Sanskrit
    (b) Sanskrit in not a language but a society
    (c) It suggest that people want to improve their status
    (d) Dalits can also read Sanskrit

14. Choose the correct statements:
   I. Sanskrit exaggerated social to mobility move up the social ladder.
   II. Sanskritization supported superiority of upper class and inferiority among lower castes.
   III. Sanskritisation seems to justify a model that rests on inequality and exclusion.
   (a) I and II
   (b) II and III
   (c) III only
   (d) All of the above

15. Among the following personalities, who are associated with paintings?
   I. Ravi Verma
   II. Chandu Menon
   III. Abanindranath Tagore
   (a) I and II
   (b) II only
   (c) I and III
   (d) All of the above

16. Choose the correct statement regarding modernization in India?
   (a) It is improvement in technology and production processes.
   (b) In India the beginnings of capitalism took place within the colonial context.
   (c) Modernization in India is quite similar to the west.
   (d) It referred to the path of development that much of west Europe or North America has taken.

17. The term 'secularism' implies -
   I. A process of decline in the influence of religion.
   II. The growth of religious consciousness and conflict has increased all over the world.
   III. It is indicated by the involvement with religious organization.
   (a) I and III
   (b) II and III
   (c) III only
   (d) All of the above

18. As sanskritisation resulted in the adoption of upper caste rites and rituals, the following were the impacts -
   I. Dowry practice in the name of culture
   II. Seclusion of girls and women
   III. Practice of caste discrimination
   (a) I and II
   (b) II and III
   (c) I and III
   (d) All of the above

19. Which of the following is correct about westernization?
   (a) It involves the imitation of external forms of culture.
   (b) It necessarily mean that people adopt modern values of democracy and equality.
   (c) Both (a) and (b)
   (d) Neither (a) nor (b)

20. The new trend of painting was carried by Raja Ravi Verma. What makes it doifferent from the traditional way of painting?
   I. Blend of flatter with two dimensions
   II. Use of water colors
   III. Use of oil to draw painting
   (a) I and II
   (b) I and III
   (c) II and III
   (d) All of the above

21. In regions where the non-Sanskritic castes were dominant, it was their influence that was stronger. This region is known as -
   (a) Secularism
   (b) Modernization
   (c) De-Sanskritization
   (d) Westernization

Answer Keys

1. (b) 2. (a) 3. (c) 4. (c) 5. (b) 6. (a) 7. (b) 8. (c) 9. (a) 10. (a)

11. (c) 12. (b) 13. (c) 14. (d) 15. (c) 16. (c) 17. (d) 18. (d) 19. (a) 20. (b)

21. (c)

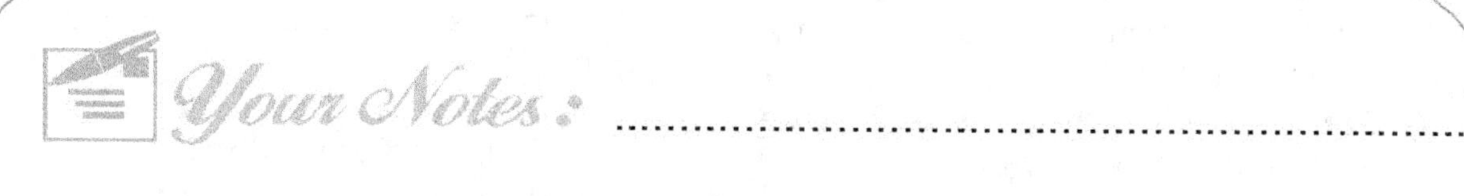
Your Notes :

Story of Indian Democracy

Chapter at Glance

The idea of democracy in India

- Democracy is a government of the people, by the people, and for the people.

- Democracies fall into two basic categories, direct and representative.

- In a direct democracy, all citizens, without the intermediary of elected or appointed officials, can participate in making public decisions.

- Ours is a representative democracy. Every citizen has the important right to vote her/his representative.

- People elect their representatives to all levels from Panchayats, Municipal Boards, State Assemblies and Parliament.

- There has increasingly been a feeling that democracy ought to involve people more regularly and should not just mean casting a vote every five years.

- Both the concepts of participatory democracy and decentralised governance have thus become popular.

- Participatory democracy is a system of democracy in which the members of a group or community participate collectively in the taking of major decisions. This chapter will discuss the panchayati raj system.

Indian Constitution

The Core Values Of Indian Democracy

- India fought for its independence from British colonialism a vision of what Indian democracy ought to look like emerged.

- As far back as in 1928, Motilal Nehru and eight other Congress leaders drafted a constitution for India.

- In 1931, the resolution at the Karachi session of the Indian National Congress dwelt on how independent India's constitution should look like.

- The Karachi Resolution reflects a vision of democracy that meant not just formal holding of elections but a substantive reworking of the Indian social structure in order to have a genuine democratic society.

- The Karachi Resolution clearly spells out the vision of democracy that the nationalist movement in India had.

- It articulates the values that were further given full expression in the Indian Constitution.

- The Preamble of the Indian Constitution seeks to ensure not just political justice but also social and economic justice.

- The equality is not just about equal political rights but also of status and opportunity.

Karachi Resolution, 1931

What Swaraj will Include?

Karachi Congress Resolution, 1931 Swaraj as conceived by the Congress should include real economic freedom of the masses. The Congress declares that no constitution will be acceptable to it unless it provides or enables the Swaraj Government to provide for:

1. Freedom of expression, association and meeting.

2. Freedom of religion.

3. Protection of all cultures and languages.

4. All citizens shall be equal before the law.

5. No disability in employment or trade or profession on account of religion, caste or sex.

6. Equal rights and duties for all in regard to public wells, schools, etc.

7. All to have right to bear arms in accordance with regulations.

8. No person to be deprived of property or liberty except in accordance with law.

9. Religious neutrality of State.

10. Adult Suffrage.

11. Free compulsory primary education.

12. No titles to be conferred.

13. Capital punishment to be abolished.

14. Freedom of movement for every citizen of India and right to settle and acquire property in any part thereof, and equal protection of law.

15. Proper standard of life for industrial workers and suitable machinery for settlement of disputes between employers and workers and protection against old age, sickness, etc.

16. All labour to be free from conditions of serfdom.

17. Special protection of women workers.

18. Children not to be employed in mines and factories.

19. Rights of peasants and workers to form unions.

20. Reform of system of land revenue and tenure and rent, exempting rent and revenue for uneconomical holdings and reduction of dues payable for smaller holdings.

21. Inheritance tax on graduated scale.

22. Reduction of military expenditure by at least half.

23. No servant of State ordinarily to be paid above Rs 500 per month.

24. Abolition of Salt tax.

25. Protection of indigenous cloth against competition of foreign cloth.

26. Total prohibition of intoxicating drinks and drugs.

27. Currency and exchange in national interest.

28. Nationalisation of key industries and services, railways, etc.

29. Relief of agricultural indebtedness and control of usury.

30. Military training for citizens.

PREAMBLE

WE, THE PEOPLE OF INDIA, having solemnly resolved to constitute India into a [SOVEREIGN SOCIALIST SECULAR DEMOCRATIC REPUBLIC] and to secure to all its citizen:

JUSTICE, social, economic and political;

LIBERTY of thought, expression, belief, faith and worship;

EQUALITY of status and opportunity;

And to promote among them all

FRATERNITY assuring the dignity of the individual and the {unity and integrity of the Nation}'   IN OUR CONSTITUENT ASSEMBLY this twenty-sixth day of November, 1949, do HEREBY ADOPT, ENACT AND GIVE TO OURSELVES THIS CONSTITUTION.

Debates in Constituent Assembly

- In 1939, Gandhiji wrote an article in the 'Harijan' called 'The Only Way' in which he said "... the Constituent Assembly alone can produce a constitution indigenous to the country and truly and fully representing the will of the people" one based on "unadulterated adult franchise for both men and women".

- The popular demand in 1939 for a Constituent Assembly was, after several ups and downs conceded by Imperialist Britain in 1945.

- In July 1946, the elections were held. In August 1946, The Indian National Congress' Expert Committee moved a resolution in the Constituent Assembly.

- This contained the declaration that India shall be a Republic where the declared social, economic and political justice will be guaranteed to all the people of India.

- On matters of social justice, there were lively debates on whether government functions should be prescribed and the state should be bound down to them.

- Issues debated ranged from right to employment, to social security, land reforms to property rights, to the organisation of panchayats.

The Constitution and Social Change

- The basic objectives laid down in the Constitution and which are generally agreed in the Indian political world as being obviously just.

- These would be empowerment of the poor and marginalised, poverty alleviation, ending of caste and positive steps to treat all groups equally.

- Competing interests do not always reflect a clear class divide.

Note: Take the issue of the close down of a factory because it emits toxic waste and affects the health of those around. This is a matter of life, which the Constitution protects. The flipside is that the closure will render people jobless. Livelihood again, is a matter of life that the Constitution protects. It is interesting that at the time of drawing up the Constitution, the Constituent Assembly was fully aware of this complexity and plurality but was intent on securing social justice as a guarantee.

Constitutional Norms And Social Justice: Interpretation To Aid Social Justice

- Law is law because it carries the means to coerce or force obedience. The power of the state is behind it.

- The basic norm from which all other rules and authorities flow is called the Constitution. It is the document that constitutes a nation's tenets.

- The Indian Constitution is India's basic norm. All other laws are made as per the procedures the Constitution prescribes.

- These laws are made and implemented by the authorities specified by the Constitution.

- A hierarchy of courts (which too are authorities created by the Constitution) interpret the laws when there is a dispute.

- The Supreme Court is the highest court and the ultimate interpreter of the Constitution.

- The Supreme Court has enhanced the substance of Fundamental Rights in the Constitution in many important ways.

  - A Fundamental Right includes all that is incidental to it.

  - The terse words of Article 21 recognising the right to life and liberty have been interpreted as including all that goes into a life of quality, including livelihood, health, shelter, education and dignity. In various pronouncements different attributes of 'life' have been expanded and 'life' has been explained to mean more than mere animal existence. These interpretations have been used to provide relief to prisoners subjected to torture and deprivation, release and rehabilitation of bonded labourers, against environmentally degrading activities, to provide primary health care and primary education.

  - In 1993 the Supreme Court held that Right to Information is part of and incidental to the Right to Expression under Article 19(1) (a).

  - Reading Directive Principles into the content of Fundamental Rights. The Supreme Court read the Directive Principle of "equal pay for equal work" into the Fundamental Right to Equality under Article 14 and has provided relief to many plantation and agricultural labourers and to others.

- The Constitution is not just a ready referencer of do's and don'ts for social justice. It has the potential for the meaning of social justice to be extended.

- Social movements have also aided the Courts and authorities to interpret the contents of rights and principles in keeping with the contemporary understanding on social justice.

- The Directive Principle on village panchayats was moved as an amendment in the Constituent Assembly by K. Santhanam. After forty odd years it became a Constitutional imperative after the 73rd Amendment in 1992.

The Panchayati Raj And The Challenges Of Rural Social Transformation

- Panchayati Raj translates literally to 'Governance by five individuals'.

- The idea is to ensure at the village or grass root level a functioning and vibrant democracy.

- When the constitution was being drafted panchayats did not find a mention in it. At this juncture, a number of members expressed their sorrow, anger and disappointment over this issue.

- The concept of local government was dear to Gandhiji too. He envisaged each village as a self-sufficient unit conducting its own affairs and saw gram-swarajya to be an ideal model to be continued after independence.

The three-tier system of Panchayati Raj Institution

- The structure is like a pyramid.

  - At the base of the structure stands the unit of democracy or Gram Sabha.

  - This consists of the entire body of citizens in a village or grama.

  - It is this general body that elects the local government and charges it with specific responsibilities.

  - The Gram Sabhas ideally ought to provide an open forum for discussions and village-level development activities and play a crucial role in ensuring inclusion of the weaker sections in the decision-making processes.

- The 73rd Amendment provided a three-tier system of Panchayati Raj for all states having a population of over twenty lakhs
- It became mandatory that election to these bodies be conducted every five years.
- It provided reservation of seats for the Scheduled Castes, Scheduled Tribes and thirty three percent seats for women.
- It constituted District Planning Committee to prepare drafts and develop plans for the district as a whole

Establishing PRIs

- In 1992 that grassroot democracy or decentralised governance was ushered in by the 73rd Constitutional Amendment.
- This act provided constitutional status to the Panchayati Raj Institutions (PRIs).
- It is compulsory now for local self-government bodies in rural and municipal areas to be elected every five years.
- The control of local resources is given to the elected local bodies.
- The 73rd and 74th amendments to the Constitution ensured the reservation of one third of the total seats for women in all elected offices of local bodies in both the rural and urban areas.
- Out of this, 17 per cent seats are reserved for women belonging to the scheduled castes and tribes.
- This amendment is significant as for the first time it brought women into elected bodies which also bestowed on them decision making powers.
- One third of the seats in local bodies, gram panchayats, village panchayats, municipalities, city corporations and district boards are reserved for women.

- A constitutional amendment prescribed a three-tier system of local self-governance for the entire country, effective since 1992-93.

Powers And Responsibilities Of Panchayats

- According to the Constitution, Panchayats should be given powers and authority to function as institutions of self-government.
- It, thus, requires all state governments to revitalise local representative institutions.
- The following powers and responsibility were delegated to the Panchayats:
  - to prepare plans and schemes for economic development
  - to promote schemes that will enhance social justice
  - to levy, collect and appropriate taxes, duties, tolls and fees
  - help in the devolution of governmental responsibilities, especially that of finances to local authorities

Social Welfare

- Social welfare responsibilities of the Panchayats include the maintenance of burning and burial grounds, recording statistics of births and deaths, establishment of child welfare and maternity centres, control of cattle pounds, propagation of family planning and promotion of agricultural activities.
- The development activities include the construction of roads, public buildings, wells, tanks and schools.
- They also promote small cottage industries and take care of minor irrigation works.
- Many government schemes like the Integrated Rural Development Programme (IRDP) and Integrated Child Development Scheme (ICDS) are monitored by members of the panchayat.

Finances

- The main income of the Panchayats is from tax levied on property, profession, animals, vehicles, cess on land revenue and rentals.
- The resources are further increased by the grants received through the Zilla Panchayat.
- It is also considered compulsory for Panchayat offices to put up boards outside their offices, listing the break up of funds received, and utilisation of the financial aid received.
- This exercise was taken up to ensure that people at the grassroot level should have the 'right to information' - opening all functioning to the public eye.

- People had the right to scrutinise allocation of money and ask reasons for decisions that were taken for the welfare and development activities of the village.

Justice

- Nyaya Panchayats have been constituted in some states. They possess the authority to hear some petty, civil and criminal cases.
- They can impose fines but cannot award a sentence.
- These village courts have often been successful in bringing about an agreement amongst contending parties.
- They have been particularly effective in punishing men who harass women for dowry and perpetrate violence against them.

Panchayati Raj In Tribal Area

- Many tribal areas have had a rich tradition of grassroot democratic functioning.
- All the three major ethnic tribal groups, namely, the Khasis, Jaintias and the Garos have their own traditional political institutions that have existed for hundreds of years.
- These political institutions were fairly well-developed and functioned at various tiers, such as the village level, clan level and state level.
- For instance, in the traditional political system of the Khasis each clan had its own council known as the 'Durbar Kur' which was presided over by the clan headman.
- Though there is a long tradition of grassroot political institutions in Meghalaya, a large chunk of tribal areas lie outside the provisions of the 73rd Amendment.
- This may be because the concerned policy makers did not wish to interfere with the traditional tribal institutions.

Political Parties, Pressure Groups And Democratic Politics

- In a democratic form of government political parties are key actors.
- A political party may be defined as an organisation oriented towards achieving legitimate control of government through an electoral process.

- Political Party is an organisation established with the aim of achieving governmental power and using that power to pursue a specific programme.
- Political parties are based on certain understanding of society and how it ought to be.
- In a democratic system the interests of different groups are also represented by political parties, who take up their case.
- Different interest groups will work towards influencing political parties.
- Interest Groups are organised to pursue specific interests in the political arena, operating primarily by lobbying the members of legislative bodies.
- In some situations, there may be political organisations which seek to achieve power but are denied the opportunity to do so through standard means.
- These organisations are best regarded as movements until they achieve recognition.
- Some argue that the concept of pressure groups underestimate the power that dominant social groups such as class, caste or gender have in society.
- They feel that it would be more accurate to suggest that dominant class or classes control the state.
- This does not negate the fact that social movements and pressure groups also continue to play a very important role in a democracy.

Some Important Groups

- Industrialists form associations such as Federation of Indian Chambers and Commerce (FICCI) and Association of Chambers of Commerce (ASSOCHAM).
- Workers form trade unions such as the Indian Trade Union Congress (INTUC) or the Centre for Indian Trade Unions (CITU).
- Farmers form agricultural unions such as Shetkari Sangathan. Agricultural labourers have their own unions.

Exercise

1. A community organization or a tribal council is an example of which of the following type of Democracy?
   (a) Direct democracy
   (b) Indirect democracy
   (c) Republican government
   (d) None of the above

2. British introduced western education to create a western educated Indian middle class. The reason was -
   (a) To prove their superiority in India
   (b) To help the colonial rulers to continue their rule
   (c) To spread Christianity by conversion
   (d) To introduce nationalism in India

3. 'Equality will be of no value without fraternity or liberty. It seems that the three can coexist only if one follows the way of the Buddha.' This statement was given by -
   (a) Mahatma Gandhi
   (b) Raja Rammohun Roy
   (c) B R Ambedkar
   (d) Subhash Chandra Bose

4. Choose the incorrect statement:
   (a) Motilal Nehru and eight other Congress leaders drafted a constitution for India in 1928.
   (b) In 1931, the Karachi resolution of the Indian National Congress dwelt on how independent India's constitution should look like.
   (c) Nehru Report reflected a vision of democracy after independence.
   (d) Karachi resolution articulates the values that were further given full expression in the Indian Constitution.

5. Equality in India is about -
   I. Political rights
   II. Status
   III. Opportunities
   (a) I and II
   (b) II and III
   (c) III only
   (d) All of the above

6. Congress declares that no constitution will be acceptable unless it provides or enables the Swaraj Government. As per Congress, Swaraj includes:
   (a) Suffrage
   (b) Real economic freedom

   (c) Secured rights to dalits
   (d) Ramrajya

7. As per Gandhiji, Constituent Assembly could produce Constitution on the basis of ....
   (a) Unadulterated adult franchise for both men and women
   (b) Social inclusion
   (c) Economic equality
   (d) Political rights

8. The resolution declared that India shall be a Republic where the declared social, economic and political justice will be guaranteed to all the people of India was moved by -
   (a) Independence Act, 1947
   (b) Indian National Congress
   (c) Gaya session of Congress
   (d) Karachi resolution

9. The right to useful employment could and should be made real by a categoric obligation on the part of the state to provide useful work to every citizen who was able and qualified. It was suggested by -
   (a) Mahatma Gandhi   (b) Jawaharlal Nehru
   (c) K T Shah   (d) B R Ambedkar

10. Which of the following are true about Directive Principals of States Policy?
    I. It was adopted by the Constituent Assembly
    II. It is enforceable in the court
    III. Constituent Assembly added the clause of organizing village panchayats
    (a) I only   (b) II and III
    (c) I and II   (d) All of the above

11. Which of the following are principals under Directive Principal of States policy?
    I. Promotion of cottage industry on cooperative lines in urban and rural areas
    II. Agriculture and animal husbandry to be organized on modern lines
    III. Village panchayat should be organized and endow with the powers and authority to be effective units of local self-government.
    (a) I and II   (b) II and III
    (c) I only   (d) All of the above

12. The issue of the close down of a factory because it emits toxic waste and affects the health of those around. What will be the impact of such action?
   (a) Right to life will be protected
   (b) Closure will render people jobless
   (c) Environment will be protected
   (d) All of the above

13. Article 21 recognises the right to life and liberty. It interprets -
   I. Livelihood   II. Dignity
   III. Shelter   IV. Education
   (a) I and IV
   (b) II, III and IV
   (c) I, II and III
   (d) All of the above

14. Right to information is part and incidental to the following:
   (a) Fundamental Right
   (b) Directive Principal of States Policy
   (c) Fundamental Duties
   (d) Preamble

15. The concept of local self-government was dear to Mahatma Gandhi as it provides -
   (a) Decentralization
   (b) Self-sufficiency in conducting its own affairs
   (c) Fight against will of upper caste
   (d) Freedom from exploitation of down trodden

16. Which of the provisions are incorporated in 73rd and 74th Amendment Act?
   I. 1/3rd seats to be reserved for women
   II. Schemes to be promoted and formulated to enhance social justice
   III. Collection of taxes and duties
   IV. Devolution of governmental responsibilities
   (a) I, II and III
   (b) II, III and IV
   (c) I, III and IV
   (d) All of the above

17. Which of the following is true regarding Nyaya Panchayats?
   I. It is constituted in every state to provide justice to everyone.
   II. It possesses the authority to hear some petty, civil and criminal cases.
   III. It can impose fines and award a sentence.
   (a) I and II
   (b) II only
   (c) II and III
   (d) All of the above

Read the following passage and answer question nos 18, 19 and 20:

Many tribal areas have had a rich tradition of grassroot democratic functioning. We give an illustrative example from Meghalaya. All the three major ethnic tribal groups, namely, the Khasis, Jaintias and the Garos have their own traditional political institutions that have existed for hundreds of years. These political institutions were fairly well-developed and functioned at various tiers, such as the village level, clan level and state level. For instance, in the traditional political system of the Khasis each clan had its own council known as the 'Durbar Kur' which was presided over by the clan headman. Though there is a long tradition of grassroot political institutions in Meghalaya, a large chunk of tribal areas lie outside the provisions of the 73rd Amendment. This may be because the concerned policy makers did not wish to interfere with the traditional tribal institutions.

18. Choose the incorrect statement about grassroot democracy in tribal areas:
   (a) Tribal areas have a rich traditional grassroot democracy.
   (b) Their traditional political institution is much older.
   (c) Political institution is multi-tiered and independent of each other.
   (d) None of the above

19. Darbar Kur in Khaisis traditional political system functions as -
   (a) The upper tier of traditional political system
   (b) Every tier has darbar kur
   (c) It is functioning as per 73rd Amendment Act.
   (d) A council presided by clan headman.

20. In Meghalaya despite of its long traditional political institution, a large chunk of tribal areas lie outside the provisions of the 73rd Amendment. The reason is -
   (a) Policy makers do not wish to interfere in the traditional institutions.
   (b) Every tribe is having its own tradition and rules.
   (c) Rise in insurgency against government.
   (d) None of the above

Answer Keys

1. (a)	2. (b)	3. (c)	4. (c)	5. (d)	6. (b)	7. (a)	8. (b)	9. (c)	10. (a)
11. (b)	12. (b)	13. (d)	14. (a)	15. (b)	16. (c)	17. (b)	18. (c)	19. (d)	20. (a)

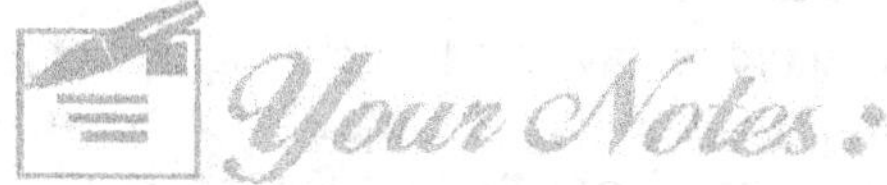 *Your Notes :* ....

CHAPTER 4

Change and Development in Rural Society

Chapter at Glance

Indian Agrarian Society

- Indian society is primarily a rural society though urbanisation is growing.
- The majority of India's people live in rural areas (69 per cent, according to the 2011 Census).
- They make their living from agriculture or related occupations.
- Agricultural land is the most important productive resource for a great many Indians.
- Land is also the most important form of property. But land is not just a 'means of production' nor just a 'form of property'. Nor is agriculture just a form of livelihood. It is also a way of life.
- Most of the New Year festivals in different regions of India - such as Pongal in Tamil Nadu, Bihu in Assam, Baisakhi in Punjab and Ugadi in Karnataka - actually celebrate the main harvest season and herald the beginning of a new agricultural season.

Agrarian Structure: Caste And Class In Rural India

- Agricultural land is the single most important resource and form of property in rural society.
- The term agrarian structure is often used to refer to the structure or distribution of landholding.
- Medium and large landowners are usually able to earn sufficient or even large incomes from cultivation.
- But agricultural labourers are more often than not paid below the statutory minimum wage and earn very little. Their incomes are low. Their employment is insecure.
- Most agricultural labourers are daily-wage workers. And do not have work for many days of the year. This is known as underemployment.
- Similarly, tenants (cultivators who lease their land from landowners) have lower incomes than owner-cultivators. Because they have to pay a substantial rent to the landowner - often as much as 50 to 75 per cent of the income from the crop.
- Agrarian society can be understood in terms of its class structure. In each region, the dominant caste is the most powerful group, economically and politically, and dominates local society.
- Examples of dominant landowning groups are the Jats and Rajputs of U.P., the Vokkaligas and Lingayats in Karnataka, Kammas and Reddis in Andhra Pradesh, and Jat Sikhs in Punjab.
- Members of low ranked caste groups had to provide labour for a fixed number of days per year to the village zamindar or landlord.
- Similarly, lack of resources, and dependence on the landed class for economic, social, and political support, meant that many of the working poor were tied to landowners in 'hereditary' labour relationships (bonded labour), such as the halpati system in Gujarat (Breman, 1974) and the jeeta system in Karnataka.
- In a village of northern Bihar, the majority of the landowners are Bhumihars, who are also the dominant caste.

The Impact of Land Reforms

The Colonial Period

- When the British colonised India, in many areas they ruled through these local zamindars. They also granted property rights to the zamindars.
- Under the British, the zamindars were given more control over land than they had before. Since the colonisers also imposed heavy land revenue (taxes) on agriculture, the zamindars extracted as much produce or money as they could out of the cultivators.

- One result of this zamindari system was that agricultural production stagnated or declined during much of the period of British rule.

- Many districts of colonial India were administered through the zamindari system. In other areas that were under direct British rule had what was called the raiyatwari system of land settlement (raiyat means cultivator in Telugu).

- In this system, the 'actual cultivators' (who were themselves often landlords and not cultivators) rather than the zamindars were responsible for paying the tax.

- Because the colonial government dealt directly with the farmers or landlords, rather than through the overlords, the burden of taxation was less and cultivators had more incentive to invest in agriculture. As a result, these areas became relatively more productive and prosperous.

Independent India

- After India became independent, Nehru and his policy advisors embarked on a programme of planned development that focused on agrarian reform as well as industrialisation.

- The policy makers were responding to the dismal agricultural situation in India at that time.

- They felt that a major reform in the agrarian structure, and especially in the landholding system and the distribution of land, was necessary if agriculture were to progress.

- The first important legislation was the abolition of the zamindari system, which removed the layer of intermediaries who stood between the cultivators and the state.

- Of all the land reform laws that were passed, this was probably the most effective, for in most areas it succeeded in taking away the superior rights of the zamindars over the land and weakening their economic and political power.

- It only removed the top layer of landlords in the multi-layered agrarian structure.

- Among the other major land reform laws that were introduced were the tenancy abolition and regulation acts.

- They attempted either to outlaw tenancy altogether or to regulate rents to give some security to the tenants.

- In most of the states, these laws were never implemented very effectively.

- In West Bengal and Kerala, there was a radical restructuring of the agrarian structure that gave land rights to the tenants.

- The third major category of land reform laws were the Land Ceiling Acts.

- These laws imposed an upper limit on the amount of land that can be owned by a particular family.

- The ceiling varies from region to region, depending on the kind of land, its productivity, and other such factors.

- Very productive land has a low ceiling while unproductive dry land has a higher ceiling limit.

- According to these acts, the state is supposed to identify and take possession of surplus land (above the ceiling limit) held by each household, and redistribute it to landless families and households in other specified categories, such as SCs and STs. But in most of the states these acts proved to be toothless.

Loopholes in the law

- Landowners managed to divide the land among relatives and others, including servants, in so-called 'benami transfers' - which allowed them to keep control over the land (in fact if not in name).

- In some places, some rich farmers divorced their wives (but continued to live with them) in order to avoid the provisions of the Land Ceiling Act, which allowed a separate share for unmarried women but not for wives.

The Green Revolution and Its Social Consequences

- The Green Revolution of the 1960s and 1970s brought about significant changes in the areas where it took place.

- It was a government programme of agricultural modernisation. It was largely funded by international agencies that was based on providing high-yielding variety (HYV) or hybrid seeds along with pesticides, fertilisers, and other inputs, to farmers.

- Green Revolution programmes were introduced only in areas that had assured irrigation, because sufficient water was necessary for the new seeds and methods of cultivation.

- It was also targeted mainly at the wheat and rice-growing areas. As a result, only certain regions such as the Punjab, western U.P., coastal Andhra Pradesh, and parts of Tamil Nadu, received the first wave of the Green Revolution package.

- Agricultural productivity increased sharply because of the new technology. India was able to become self-sufficient in foodgrain production for the first time in decades.

- The Green Revolution has been considered a major achievement of the government and of the scientists who contributed to the effort.

- However, there were certain negative social effects that were pointed out by sociologists who studied the Green Revolution areas, as well as adverse environmental impacts.

Social Impacts

- It was primarily the medium and large farmers who were able to benefit from the new technology.

- This was because inputs were expensive, and small and marginal farmers could not afford to spend as much as large farmers to purchase these inputs.

- Inequality increased: Thus, in the first phase of the Green Revolution, in the 1960s and 1970s, the introduction of new technology seemed to be increasing inequalities in rural society.

- Green Revolution crops were highly profitable, mainly because they yielded more produce.

- Well-to-do farmers who had access to land, capital, technology, and know-how, and those who could invest in the new seeds and fertilisers, could increase their production and earn more money.

- In many cases it led to the displacement of tenant-cultivators

- This made the rich farmers better off, and worsened the condition of the landless and marginal holders.

- Rural to urban migration: In addition, the introduction of machinery such as tillers, tractors, threshers, and harvesters (in areas such as Punjab and parts of Madhya Pradesh) led to the displacement of the service caste groups who used to carry out these agriculture-related activities. This process of displacement also increased the pace of rural-urban migration.

- Worsened economic condition: The ultimate outcome of the Green Revolution was a process of 'differentiation', in which the rich grew richer and many of the poor stagnated or grew poorer.

- It should be noted that employment and wages for agricultural workers did increase in many areas, because the demand for labour increased.

- Moreover, rising prices and a shift in the mode of payment of agricultural workers from payment in kind (grain) to cash, actually worsened the economic condition of most rural workers.

Second phase of Green Revolution

- The second phase of the Green Revolution which began in 1980s, farmers living in the dry and semi-arid regions of India began following Green Revolution cultivation practices.

- In these areas there has been a significant shift from dry to wet (irrigated) cultivation, along with changes in the cropping pattern and type of crops grown.

- Increasing commercialisation and dependence on the market in these areas (for instance, where cotton cultivation has been promoted) has increased rather than reduced livelihood insecurity, as farmers who once grew food for consumption now depend on the market for the incomes.

- In marketoriented cultivation, especially where a single crop is grown, a fall in prices or a bad crop can spell financial ruin for farmers.

- In most of the Green Revolution areas, farmers have switched from a multi-crop system, which allowed them to spread risks, to a mono-crop regime, which means that there is nothing to fall back on in case of crop failure.

- Another negative outcome of the Green Revolution strategy was the worsening of regional inequalities.

- The areas that underwent this technological transformation became more developed while other areas stagnated.

- For instance, the Green Revolution was promoted more in the western and southern parts of the country, and in Punjab, Haryana, and western U.P., than in the eastern parts of the country (Das, 1999).

Transformations in Rural Society After Independence

- Several profound transformations in the nature of social relations in rural areas took place in the post-Independence period, especially in those regions that underwent the Green Revolution. These included:

  - an increase in the use of agricultural labour as cultivation became more intensive;

  - a shift from payment in kind (grain) to payment in cash;

  - a loosening of traditional bonds or hereditary relationships between farmers or landowners and agricultural workers (known as bonded labour)

  - the rise of a class of 'free' wage labourers.

- The transformation in labour relations is regarded by some scholars as indicative of a transition to capitalist agriculture. Because the capitalist mode of production is based on the separation of the workers from the means of production (in this case, land), and the use of 'free' wage labour.

- As cultivation became more commercialised, these rural areas were also becoming integrated to the wider economy. This process increased the flow of money into villages and expanding opportunities for business and employment.

- The state invested in the development of rural infrastructure, such as irrigation facilities, roads and electricity, and on the provision of agricultural inputs, including credit through banks and cooperatives.
- The recently launched Deen Dayal Upadhyaya Gram Jyoti Yojana is an effort of the Indian government in this direction. The overall outcome of these efforts at 'rural development' was not only to transform the rural economy and agriculture, but also the agrarian structure and the rural society itself.
- One way in which rural social structure was altered by agricultural development since the 1960s was through the enrichment of the medium and large farmers who adopted the new technologies.
- In several agriculturally rich regions, such as coastal Andhra Pradesh, western Uttar Pradesh, and central Gujarat, well-to-do farmers belonging to the dominant castes began to invest their profits from agriculture in other types of business ventures.

Circulation Of Labour

- As 'traditional' bonds of patronage between labourers or tenants and landlords broke down, and as the seasonal demand for agricultural labour increased in prosperous Green Revolution regions such as the Punjab, a pattern of seasonal migration emerged in which thousands of workers circulate between their home villages and more prosperous areas where there is more demand for labour and higher wages.
- Migrant workers come mainly from drought-prone and less productive regions, and they go to work for part of the year on farms in the Punjab and Haryana, or on brick kilns in U.P., or construction sites in cities such as New Delhi or Bangalore.
- These migrant workers have been termed 'footloose labour' by Jan Breman, but this does not imply freedom.
- Migration and lack of job security have created very poor working and living conditions for these workers.
- Women are also emerging as the main source of agricultural labour, leading to the 'feminisation of agricultural labour force.' The insecurity of women is greater because they earn lower wages than men for similar work.
- While women toil on the land as landless labourers and as cultivators, the prevailing patrilineal kinship system, and other cultural practices that privilege male rights, largely exclude women from land ownership.

Globalisation, Liberalisation, And Rural Society

- The policy of liberalisation that India has been following since the late 1980s have had a very significant impact on agriculture and rural society.
- The policy entails participation in the World Trade Organisation (WTO), which aims to bring about a more free international trading system and requires the opening up of Indian markets to imports.

Contract Farming

- In 'contract farming' systems, the company identifies the crop to be grown, provides the seeds and other inputs, as well as the know-how and often also the working capital.
- In return, the farmer is assured of a market because the company guarantees that it will purchase the produce at a predetermined fixed price.
- Contract farming is very common now in the production of specialised items such as cut flowers, fruits such as grapes, figs and pomegranates, cotton, and oilseeds.
- While contract farming appears to provide financial security to farmers, it can also lead to greater insecurity as farmers become dependent on these companies for their livelihoods.
- Contract farming of export-oriented products such as flowers and gherkins also means that agricultural land is diverted away from food grain production.
- Contract farming has sociological significance in that it disengages many people from the production process and makes their own indigenous knowledge of agriculture irrelevant.

Entry of MNCs

- Another, and more widespread aspect of the globalisation of agriculture is the entry of multinationals into this sector as sellers of agricultural inputs such as seeds, pesticides, and fertilisers.
- Over the last decade or so, the government has scaled down its agricultural development programmes, and 'agricultural extension' agents have been replaced in the villages by agents of seed, fertiliser, and pesticide companies.
- This has led to the increased dependence of farmers on expensive fertilisers and pesticides, which has reduced their profits, put many farmers into debt, and also created an ecological crisis in rural areas.

Consequences: Issue of Farmer's Suicide

- While farmers in India for centuries have periodically faced distress due to drought, crop failures, or debt,

- the phenomenon of farmers' suicides appears to be new.
- Sociologists have attempted to explain this phenomenon by looking at the structural and social changes that have been occurring in agriculture and agrarian society.
- Many farmers, who have committed suicide were marginal farmers, who were attempting to increase their productivity, primarily by practising Green Revolution methods.
- However, undertaking such production meant facing several risks: the cost of production has increased tremendously due to a decrease in agricultural subsidies, the markets are not stable, and many farmers borrow heavily in order to invest in expensive inputs and improve their production.
- The loss of either the crop (due to spread of disease or pests, excessive rainfall, or drought), and in some cases, lack of an adequate support or market price means that farmers are unable to bear the debt burden or sustain their families.
- Such distress is compounded by the changing culture in rural areas, in which increased incomes are required for marriages, dowries and to sustain new activities and expenses, such as education and medical care.
- Suicides of farmers is basically associated with debt, as well as, natural disasters, resulting in the failure of agricutural produce.
- Pradhan Mantri Fasal Bima Yojana, Gram Uday se Bharat Uday Abhiyan and National Rurban Mission are some of the schemes of the Government of India, which may provide unified help to farmers all over the country.

Exercise

1. **Assertion (A):** Land is a way of life.

   Reason (R): Many of our cultural practices and patterns can be traced to our agrarian backgrounds.
   (a) Both A and R are true and R is the correct explanation of A.
   (b) Both A and R are true and R is not the correct explanation of A.
   (c) A is true and R is false
   (d) A is false and R is true

2. Pongal, Bihu, Ugadi festivals are celebrated in different parts of India. These festivals are celebrating as -
   (a) New year   (b) Harvest season
   (c) Religious festival   (d) Folk and tribal festival

3. Which of following are true about transformation in rural society after independence?
   I.   Use of agricultural labour increased as cultivation became more intensive
   II. Change in the mode of payment
   III. Rise in the 'free' wage labor class
   (a) I and II   (b) II and III
   (c) I and III   (d) All of the above

4. The single most important resource and form of property in rural society is -
   (a) Agricultural land
   (b) Farm produce
   (c) Kharif and Rabi crop production
   (d) Availability of labor

5. Which of the pairs are correct regarding landowning class?
   (a) Jat Sikhs: Punjab and Haryana
   (b) Vokkaligas: Karnataka
   (c) Kammas: Andhra and Kerala
   (d) Rajputs: Uttar Pradesh

6. Halpati system in Gujarat and Jeeta system of Karnataka is an example of:
   (a) Hereditary landownership
   (b) Agricultural structure of society
   (c) Bonded labor
   (d) Crop cultivation technology

7. Which of the statements is correct about Raiyatwari system of land settlement?

  I. The 'actual cultivators' were landlords who had to pay taxes directly to the authority.

  II. The burden of taxation was less and cultivators had more incentive to invest in agriculture.

  III. The implemented areas became more prosperous and productive.

  (a) I and III   (b) II and III

  (c) I and II   (d) All of the above

8. Which of the following is correct chronological order of legislation?

  (a) Tenancy abolition and regulation acts - Abolition of the zamindari system - Land Ceiling Acts

  (b) Land Ceiling Acts - Abolition of the zamindari system - Tenancy abolition and regulation acts

  (c) Abolition of the zamindari system - Tenancy abolition and regulation acts - Land Ceiling Acts

  (d) Tenancy abolition and regulation acts - Land Ceiling Acts - Abolition of the zamindari system

9. Which of the following is correct about Green Revolution?

  I. It was an agricultural modernization programme

  II. It was funded by international agencies to provide HYV seeds

  III. It was introduced in areas having assured irrigation

  (a) II only   (b) II and III

  (c) I and II   (d) All of the above

10. Which of the following regions were part of Green Revolution?

  I. Andhra Pradesh including Telangana region

  II. Punjab

  III. Western Uttar Pradesh

  IV. Tamil Nadu

  (a) I, II and III

  (b) II, III and IV

  (c) I and II

  (d) All of the above

11. Which of the statement is correct?

  (a) Green Revolution made India self-sufficient in foodgrain production for the first time in decades.

  (b) Small, medium and large landholders were benefitted by the Green Revolution.

  (c) Green Revolution promoted subsistence farming.

  (d) Green Revolution brought equality among the farmers through increased production.

12. Which of the following are impact of Green Revolution?

  I. It displaced the service caste groups who used to carry out these agriculture-related activities.

  II. Farmers who were able to produce a surplus for the market were able to reap the most benefits.

  III. It increased employment and wages for agricultural workers due to increase in demand for labour.

  (a) II and III   (b) III only

  (c) I and II   (d) All of the above

13. Which of the statement is correct regarding second phase of Green Revolution?

  (a) It was taken up in dry and semi-arid regions of India.

  (b) Framers switched to multi-crop system

  (c) Due to commercialization livelihood insecurity has reduced.

  (d) None of the above

14. Green Revolution brought changes in the labor pattern, what was this?

  (a) It led to increase immigration of labors

  (b) 'Traditional' bonds of patronage between labourers or tenants and landlords broke down

  (c) It increased the seasonal demand of labors in prosperous regions.

  (d) None of the above

15. Migrant workers are also to be known as -

  (a) Unorganized workers (b)   Job seekers

  (c) Free workers   (d) Footloose labor

16. The policy of liberalisation brought by WTO that India has been following since the late 1980s have had a very significant impact on agriculture and rural society. What was the aim of the policy?

  I. Free international trading system

  II. Opening up of Indian markets to import

  III. Increase competition among farmers to increase commercialization

  (a) I and II   (b) II and III

  (c) III only   (d) All of the above

17. Choose the correct statement regarding contract farming:
    (a) Companies issue a list of crops and provide market for the same after harvest.
    (b) Company identifies the crop to be grown, provides the seeds and other inputs and the working capital.
    (c) Farmers gets financial security as they get the money during signing of contract.
    (d) All of the above

18. Which of the following are reasons of farmer's suicide in India?
    I. Debt
    II. Natural disasters
    III. Stubble burning
    (a) II and III (b) III only
    (c) I and II (d) All of the above

19. **Assertion (A):** The phenomenon of farmers' suicides in India appears to be new.
    Reason (R): The structural and social changes have been occurring in agriculture and agrarian society.
    (a) Both A and R are true and R is the correct explanation of A.
    (b) Both A and R are true and R is not the correct explanation of A.
    (c) A is true and R is false
    (d) A is false and R is true

20. Why farmer's suicide is very common phenomenon among marginal farmers?
    (a) Due to crop failure
    (b) Debt burden due to farm's input and marriages
    (c) Risk associated with the Green Revolution practice
    (d) Non-availability of market for production

Answer Keys

1. (a)	2. (a)	3. (d)	4. (a)	5. (b)	6. (c)	7. (d)	8. (c)	9. (d)	10. (b)
11. (a)	12. (d)	13. (a)	14. (c)	15. (d)	16. (a)	17. (b)	18. (c)	19. (a)	20. (c)

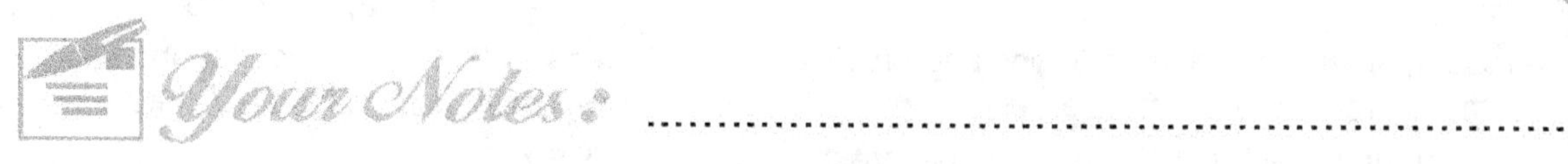

Your Notes :

Change and Development in Industrial Society

Chapter at Glance

Images Of Industrial Society

- Karl Marx, Max Weber and Emile Durkheim associated a number of social features with industry, such as urbanisation, the loss of face-to-face relationships that were found in rural areas where people worked on their own farms or for a landlord they knew, and their substitution by anonymous professional relationships in modern factories and workplaces.

- People often do not see the end result of their work because they are producing only one small part of a product. The work is often repetitive and exhausting.

- Yet, even this is better than having no work at all, i.e., being unemployed. Marx called this situation alienation, when people do not enjoy work, and see it as something they have to do only in order to survive, and even that survival depends on whether the technology has room for any human labour.

- Industrialisation leads to greater equality, at least in some spheres.

- And even as social inequalities are reducing, economic or income inequality is growing in the world.

- Often social inequality and income inequality overlap, for example, in the domination of upper caste men in well-paying professions like medicine, law or journalism. Women often get paid less than men for similar work.

Industrialisation In India

The Specificity Of Indian Industrialisation

Distribution of workers in India by employment status, 1972–2019

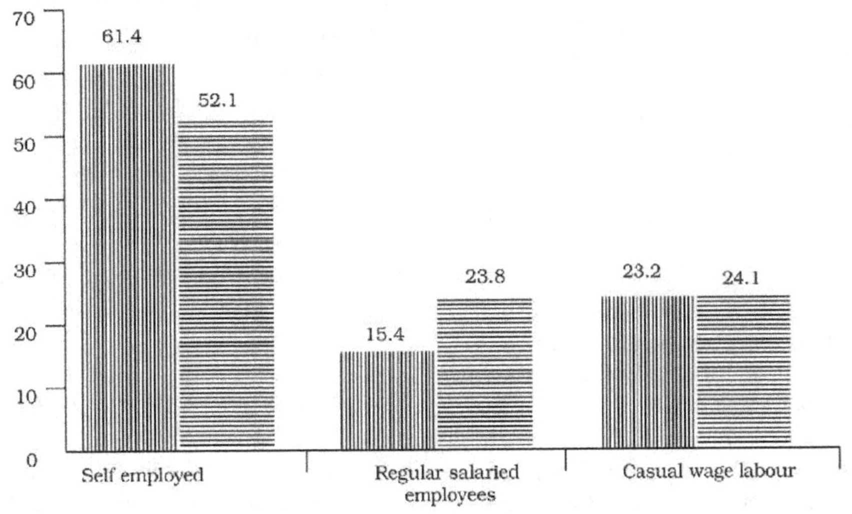

- In India, in 2018-19, nearly 43% were employed in the primary sector (agriculture and mining), 17% in the secondary sector (manufacturing, construction and utilities), and 32% in the tertiary sector (trade, transport, financial services etc.)

- The contribution of these sectors to economic growth, the share of agriculture has declined sharply, and services contribute approximately more than half.

- This is a very serious situation because it means that the sector where the maximum people are employed is not able to generate much income for them. In India, in 2018-19 the share of employment in agriculture was 42.5%, in mining and quarriying 0.4%, in manufacturing it was 12.1%, in trade, hotel and restaurant it was 12.6%, in transport, storage, communication it was 5.9%, in community, social and personal services it was 13.8%.

- In India, over 52% of the workers are self-employed, only about 24% are in regular salaried employment, while approximately 24% are in casual labour.

Organized and Unorganized Sector

- Economists and others often make a distinction between the organised or formal and unorganised or informal sector.

- There is a debate over how to define these sectors.

- According to one definition, the organised sector consists of all units employing ten or more people throughout the year.

- These have to be registered with the government to ensure that their employees get proper salaries or wages, pension and other benefits.

- In India, over 90% of the work, whether it is in agriculture, industry or services is in the unorganised or informal sector

Social Implications of Small Size of Organized Sector

I.   Very few people have the experience of employment in large firms where they get to meet people from other regions and backgrounds. Urban settings do provide some corrective to this - your neighbours in a city may be from a different place - but by and large, work for most Indians is still in small-scale workplaces.

II. Very few Indians have access to secure jobs with benefits. Of those who do, two-thirds work for the government. This is why people strive hard to get into government jobs. The rest are forced to depend on their children in their old age.

III. Very few people are members of unions, a feature of the organised sector, the unorganised or informal sector workers do not have the experience of collectively fighting for proper wages and safe working conditions.

Industrialisation In The Early Years Of Indian Independence

- The first modern industries in India were cotton, jute, coal mines and railways.

- After independence, the government took over the 'commanding heights of the economy.'

- This involved defence, transport and communication, power, mining and other projects which only government had the power to do, and which was also necessary for private industry to flourish.

- In India's mixed economy policy, some sectors were reserved for government, while others were open to the private sector.

- But within that, the government tried to ensure, through its licensing policy, that industries were spread over different regions.

- Before independence, industries were located mainly in the port cities like Madras, Bombay, Calcutta (now, Chennai, Mumbai and Kolkata, respectively).

- But since then, we see that places like Baroda, Coimbatore, Bengaluru, Pune, Faridabad and Rajkot have become important industrial centres.

- The government also tried to encourage the small-scale sector through special incentives and assistance.

- Many items like paper and wood products, stationery, glass and ceramics were reserved for the small-scale sector. In 1991, large-scale industry employed only 28 per cent of the total workforce engaged in manufacture, while the small-scale and traditional industry employed 72 per cent.

Globalisation, Liberalisation And Changes In Indian Industry

- Since the 1990s, however, the government has followed a policy of liberalisation.

- Private companies, especially foreign firms, are encouraged to invest in sectors earlier reserved for the government, including telecom, civil aviation, power etc.

- Licenses are no longer required to open industries. Foreign products are now easily available in Indian shops.

- As a result of liberalisation, many Indian companies- small and large, have been bought over by multinationals.

- At the same time some Indian companies are becoming multinational companies.

- The next major area of liberalisation is in retail.
- The government is trying to sell its share in several public sector companies, a process which is known as disinvestment.
- Many government workers are scared that after disinvestment, they will lose their jobs. In Modern Foods, which was set up by the government to make healthy bread available at cheap prices, and which was the first company to be privatised, 60% of the workers were forced to retire in the first five years.
- India is still largely an agricultural country.
- The service sector - shops, banks, the IT industry, hotels and other services are employing more people and the urban middle class is growing, along with urban middle class values like those we see in television serials and films.
- But we also see that very few people in India have access to secure jobs, with even the small number in regular salaried employment becoming more insecure due to the rise in contract labour.
- At the same time as secure employment in large industry is declining, the government is embarking on a policy of land acquisition for industry.
- These industries do not necessarily provide employment to the people of the surrounding areas, but they cause major pollution.
- Many farmers, especially adivasis, who constitute approximately 40% of those displaced, are protesting at the low rates of compensation and the fact that they will be forced to become casual labour living and working on the footpaths of India's big cities.

How People Find Jobs

- Only a small percentage of people get jobs through advertisements or through the employment exchange.
- People who are self-employed, like plumbers, electricians and carpenters at one end and teachers who give private tuitions, architects and freelance photographers at the other end, all rely on personal contacts.
- Job recruitment as a factory worker takes a different pattern. In the past, many workers got their jobs through contractors or jobbers.
- In the Kanpur textile mills, these jobbers were known as mistris, and were themselves workers.
- They came from the same regions and communities as the workers, but because they had the owner's backing they bossed over the workers.
- On the other hand, the mistri also put community-related pressures on the worker.

- Nowadays, the importance of the jobber has come down, and both management and unions play a role in recruiting their own people.
- Many workers also expect that they can pass on their jobs to their children. Many factories employ badli workers who substitute for regular permanent workers who are on leave.
- This is called contract work in the organised sector.
- Employment opportunities have two important components:

    (i) job in an organisation as a casual wage labourer or regular salaried

    (ii) Self-employment

- Recently the Government of India floated many schemes such as MUDRA, Aatmanirbhar Bharat or 'Make in India' by which hired wage works and self-employment will become possible.
- These schemes are expected to support all sections including the marginalised sections of the society, like SC, ST and other backward classes.

In case of Unorganized Sector

- The contractor system is most visible in the hiring of casual labour for work at construction sites, brickyards, and so on.
- The contractor goes to villages and asks if people want work. He will loan them some money. This loan includes the cost of transport to the work site.
- The loaned money is treated as an advance wage and the worker works without wages until the loan is repaid.
- In the past, agricultural labourers were tied to their landlord by debt. Now, however, by moving to casual industrial work, while they are still in debt, they are not bound by other social obligations to the contractor.
- In that sense, they are more free in an industrial society. They can break the contract and find another employer. Sometimes, whole families migrate and the children help their parents.

How Is Work Carried Out?

- The basic task of a manager is to control workers and get more work out of them. There are two main ways of making workers produce more.
- One is to extend the working hours. The other is to increase the amount that is produced within a given time period.
- Machinery helps to increase production, but it also creates the danger that eventually machines will replace workers.
- Both Marx and Mahatma Gandhi saw mechanisation as a danger to employment.

- Another way of increasing output is by organising work. An American called Frederick Winslow Taylor invented a new system in the 1890s, which he called 'Scientific Management'. It is also known as Taylorism or industrial engineering.

- The more mechanised an industry gets, the fewer people are employed, but they too have to work at the pace of the machine.

- One important debate in sociology is whether industrialisation and the shift to services and knowledge-based work, like IT, leads to greater skills in society. We often hear the phrase 'knowledge economy' to describe the growth of IT sector in India.

- The famous sociologist, Harry Braverman, argues that the use of machinery actually deskills workers.

Working Conditions

- The government has passed a number of laws to regulate working conditions.

- Coal mines alone employ 5.5 lakh workers. The Mines Act 1952, which has now been included in the Occupational Safety, Health and Working Condition Code, 2020, specifies the maximum number of hours a person can be made to work in a week, the need to pay overtime for any extra hours worked and safety rules.

- These rules may be followed in big companies, but not in smaller mines and quarries. Moreover, sub-contracting is widespread. Many contractors do not maintain proper registers of workers, thus avoiding any responsibility for accidents and benefits.

- After mining has finished in an area, the company is supposed to cover up the open holes and restore the area to its earlier condition. But they don't do this.

- Workers in underground mines face very dangerous conditions, due to flooding, fire, the collapse of roofs and sides, the emission of gases and ventilation failures.

- Many workers develop breathing problems and diseases like tuberculosis and silicosis.

- Those working in overground mines have to work in both hot sun and rain, and face injuries due to mine blasting, falling objects etc.

- The rate of mining accidents in India is very high compared to other countries.

- In many industries, the workers are migrants. The fish processing plants along the coastline employ mostly single young women from Tamil Nadu, Karnataka and Kerala. Ten-twelve of them are housed in small rooms, and sometimes one shift has to make way for another.

Home-Based Work

- Home-based work is an important part of the economy. This includes the manufacture of lace, zari or brocade, carpets, bidis, agarbattis and many such products. This work is mainly done by women and children.

- An agent provides raw materials and also picks up the finished product. Home workers are paid on a piece-rate basis, depending on the number of pieces they make.

An example of Bidi Industry

- The process of making bidis starts in forested villages where villagers pluck tendu leaves and sell it to the forest department or a private contractor who in turn sells it to the forest department.

- On average a person can collect 100 bundles (of 50 leaves each) a day. The government then auctions the leaves to bidi factory owners who give it to the contractors.

- The contractor in turn supplies tobacco and leaves to home-based workers. These workers, mostly women, roll the bidis - first dampening the leaves, then cutting them, filling in tobacco evenly and then tying them with thread.

- The contractor picks up these bidis and sells them to the manufacturer who roasts them, and puts on his own brand label.

- The manufacturer then sells them to a distributor who distributes the packed bidis to wholesalers who in turn sell to your neighbourhood pan shops.

Strikes And Unions

- Many workers are part of trade unions. Trade unions in India have to overcome a number of problems, such as regionalism and casteism.

- In response to harsh working conditions, sometimes workers went on strike. In a strike, workers do not go to work.

- In a lockout the management shuts the gate and prevents workers from coming.

- To call a strike is a difficult decision as managers may try to use substitute labour.

- Workers also find it hard to sustain themselves without wages.

- The famous strike of the Bombay Textile strike of 1982, which was led by the trade union leader, Dr. Datta Samant, and affected nearly a quarter of a million workers and their families.

- The strike lasted nearly two years. The workers wanted better wages and also wanted the right to form their own union.

- According to the Bombay Industrial Relations Act (BIRA), a union had to be 'approved' and the only way it could be 'approved' was if it gave up the idea of strikes.
- The Congress-led Rashtriya Mill Mazdoor Sangh (RMMS) was the only approved union and it helped to break the strike by bringing in other workers.
- The government also refused to listen to the workers' demands. Slowly after two years, people started going back to work because they were desperate.

- Nearly one lakh workers lost their jobs and went back to their villages, or took up casual labour, others moved to smaller towns, like Bhiwandi, Malegaon and Icchalkaranji, to work in the powerloom sector. Mill owners did not invest in machinery and modernisation.
- Today, they are trying to sell off the mill land to real estate dealers to build luxury apartments.

Exercise

1. Which of the following are features of organized sector?
   I. It consists of all units employing ten or more people in a month.
   II. They are registered with the government.
   III. They ensure proper salaries or wages, pension and other benefits to employees.
   (a) I only
   (b) II and III
   (c) I and II
   (d) All of the above

2. Choose the incorrect statement:
   (a) Bhilai Steel Plant does not see any riots as it is having employees from particular religion.
   (b) Bhilai Steel Plant is a public sector enterprise.
   (c) Government jobs have overcome the problem of caste discrimination.
   (d) People gets salaries and benefits in government jobs.

3. Which of the following are first modern industries in India?
   I. Cotton
   II. Jute
   III. Coal mines
   IV. Railways
   (a) I, II and IV
   (b) II, III and IV
   (c) I, III and IV
   (d) All of the above

4. Paper, wood and ceramics are reserved for which of the following sectors?
   (a) Organized sectors
   (b) Large entity sector
   (c) Small and medium sectors
   (d) Unorganized sectors

5. Which of the following were the areas where liberalization focused in India in initial years?
   (a) Small and medium sector
   (b) Retail
   (c) Banking
   (d) Real estate

6. What are the issues faced by the small companies in India?
   I. Low wages
   II. Poor working conditions
   III. Difficulty in forming trade unions
   IV. Lock out are not valid
   (a) I, II and III
   (b) II, III and IV
   (c) I, III and IV
   (d) All of the above

7. The secure employment in large industry is declining, the reason is -
   (a) Land acquisition
   (b) No employment to people in surrounding area
   (c) Both A and B
   (d) Neither A nor B

8. 'Mistris' and 'Badli' are a type of -
   (a) Factories
   (b) Mechanical engineers
   (c) Hotel staffs
   (d) Factory workers

9. Which of the following are components of employment opportunities?
   I. Job as casual labor
   II. Job in an organization and regular salaried
   III. Self-employment
   (a) I and II
   (b) II and III
   (c) I and III
   (d) All of the above

10. According to Marx and Mahatama Gandhi, which mechanism is dangerous to employment?
    (a) Hiring and firing of labors
    (b) Machinery to replace labor
    (c) More labors in unorganized sector
    (d) Low wages to the labors

11. Which of the following are correct provisions of Occupational Safety, Health and Working Condition Code, 2020?

    I. Fixing the maximum number of hours of work in a week

    II. Overtime to be paid for the extra hour works

    III. Fixing the limits of wages to be given to the workers

    (a) I and II   (b) III only

    (c) II and III   (d) All of the above

Read the following passage and answer the following questions 12, 13 and 14:

Workers in underground mines face very dangerous conditions, due to flooding, fire, the collapse of roofs and sides, the emission of gases and ventilation failures. Many workers develop breathing problems and diseases like tuberculosis and silicosis. Those working in overground mines have to work in both hot sun and rain, and face injuries due to mine blasting, falling objects etc. The rate of mining accidents in India is very high compared to other countries.

12. Working condition in underground is dangerous as it leads -

    (a) Loss of jobs

    (b) Loss of vision

    (c) Poor health condition

    (d) All of the above

13. Tuberculosis and silicosis are breathing problem which affects -

    (a) Immune system

    (b) Lungs

    (c) Eyes

    (d) Nostril and throat

14. Which of the following common issues which employees faces in the mining sites?

    I. Explosion of mines

    II. Flooding

    III. Heavy rain

    IV. Exposure to dust

    (a) I, II and III   (b) II, III and IV

    (c) I, II and IV   (d) All of the above

15. Which of the following comes in the category of home-based work?

    I. Agarbatti

    II. Carpet and lace

    III. Plastic products

    (a) I and III   (b) II and III

    (c) I and II   (d) None of the above

16. Which of the following statements is correct about lock out?

    (a) Workers do not go to work in the factories

    (b) The management shuts the gate and prevents workers from coming.

    (c) Workers forms their union and demand for wages

    (d) None of the above

17. The Bombay Textile strike of 1982 was lead by which trade union leader?

    (a) Jayprakash Bhilare

    (b) Lakshmi Bhatkar

    (c) Kisan Salunke

    (d) Dr. Datta Samant

18. According to the Bombay Industrial Relations Act (BIRA), a union had to be 'approved', if -

    (a) They put their demands peacefully

    (b) They do not disturb the management unnecessarily

    (c) They give up the idea of strike

    (d) All of the above

19. Which of the following sector of economy is known as 'knowledge economy'?

    (a) IT sector   (b) Banking sector

    (c) Education sector   (d) Organized sector

20. Which sociologist has viewed as 'the use of machinery actually deskills workers'?

    (a) Karl Marx   (b) Max Weber

    (c) Harry Braverman   (d) Emile Durkheim

Answer Keys

1. (b)	2. (a)	3. (d)	4. (c)	5. (b)	6. (a)	7. (c)	8. (d)	9. (d)	10. (b)
11. (a)	12. (c)	13. (b)	14. (d)	15. (c)	16. (b)	17. (d)	18. (c)	19. (a)	20. (c)

CHAPTER 6

Globalisation and Social Change

Chapter at Glance

- With the opening up of the market and removal of restrictions to the import of many products we have many more products from different corners of the world in our neighbourhood shops.
- Since April 1, 2001, all types of quantitative restrictions (QR) on imports were withdrawn. It is no surprise now to find a Chinese pear, an Australian apple vying for attention in the local fruit stall.
- The neighbourhood store also has Australian orange juice and ready to fry chips in frozen packets.
- What we eat and drink at home with our family and friends slowly changes. The same set of policy changes affects consumers and producers differently.
- These changes are personal because they affect individuals' lives and lifestyles.
- They are obviously also linked to public policies adopted by the government and its agreement with the World Trade Organisation (WTO).
- The dramatic changes in the media are perhaps the most visible effect of globalization.

Effects

- The effect of globalisation is far reaching. It affects us all but affects us differently.
- Thus, while for some it may mean new opportunities, for others the loss of livelihood.
- Women silk spinners and twisters of Bihar lost their jobs once the Chinese and Korean silk yarn entered the market.
- Weavers and consumers prefer this yarn as it is somewhat cheaper and has a shine. Similar displacements have come with the entry of large fishing vessels into Indian waters.
- These vessels take away the fish that used to be earlier collected by Indian fishing vessels. The livelihood of women fish sorters, dryers, vendors and net makers thereby get affected.
- In Gujarat, women gum collectors, who were picking from the 'julifera' (Baval trees), lost their employment due to the import of cheaper gum from Sudan.
- In almost all cities of India, the rag pickers lost some of their employment due to import of waste paper from developed countries.

Are Global Interconnections New To World And To India

The early years: India was not isolated from the world even two thousand years ago. Centuries ago, the famous Silk route connected India to the great civilisations, which existed in China, Persia, Egypt and Rome.

- Since India's long past, people from different parts came here, sometimes as traders, sometimes as conquerors, sometimes as migrants in search of new lands and settled down here.
- Global interactions or even a global outlook are thus not novel developments unique to the modern period or unique to modern India.

Colonialism And The Global Connection: Colonialism was part of the system that required new sources of capital, raw materials, energy, markets and a global network that sustained it.

- Often globalisation today identifies large-scale movement of people or migration as a defining feature.

Independent India And The World: Independent India retained a global outlook. In many senses this was inherited from the Indian nationalist movement.

- Commitment to liberation struggles throughout the world, solidarity with people from different parts of the world was very much part of this vision.
- Many Indians travelled overseas for education and work.

- Migration was an ongoing process.
- Export and import of raw material, goods and technology was very much part of development since independence. Foreign firms did operate in India.

Understanding Globalisation

- Globalisation refers to the growing interdependence between different people, regions and countries in the world as social and economic relationships come to stretch world-wide.
- Although economic forces are an integral part of globalisation, it would be wrong to suggest that they alone produce it.
- It has been driven forward above all by the development of information and communication technologies that have intensified the speed and scope of interaction between people all over the world.

The Different Dimensions Of Globalisation

- **Economic Dimension**

a. The Economic Policy of Liberalisation

- Globalisation involves a stretching of social and economic relationships throughout the world.
- Very broadly this process in India is termed liberalisation. The term liberalisation refers to a range of policy decisions that the Indian state took since 1991 to open up the Indian economy to the world market.
- This marked a break with an earlier stated policy of the government to have a greater control over the economy.
- The state after independence had put in place a large number of laws that ensured that the Indian market and Indian indigenous business were protected from competition of the wider world.
- The underlying assumption of such a policy was that an erstwhile colonial country would be at a disadvantage in a free market situation.
- The state also believed that the market alone would not be able to look after all the welfare of the people, particularly its disadvantaged sections.
- It felt that the state had an important role to play for the welfare of the people.
- Liberalisation of the economy meant the steady removal of the rules that regulated Indian trade and finance regulations. These measures are also described as economic reforms.
- Since July 1991, the Indian economy has witnessed a series of reforms in all major sectors of the economy (agriculture, industry, trade, foreign investment and technology, public sector, financial institutions etc).
- The basic assumption was that greater integration into the global market would be beneficial to Indian economy.

- **Economic reforms and IMF**

- The process of liberalisation also involved the taking of loans from international institutions such as the International Monetary Fund (IMF).
- These loans are given on certain conditions. The government makes commitments to pursue certain kind of economic measures that involve a policy of structural adjustments.
- These adjustments usually mean cuts in state expenditure on the social sector such as health, education and social security.
- There is also a greater say by international institutions such as the World Trade Organisation (WTO).

b. The transnational corporations

- Among the many economic factors driving globalisation, the role of transnational corporations (TNCs) is particularly important.
- TNCs are companies that produce goods or market services in more than one country.
- These may be relatively small firms with one or two factories outside the country in which they are based.
- They could also be gigantic international ones whose operations crisscross the globe.
- Some of the biggest MNCs are companies known all around the world: Coca Cola, General Motors, Colgate-Palmolive, Kodak, Mitsubishi and many others.
- They are oriented to the global markets and global profits even if they have a clear national base. Some Indian corporations are also becoming transnational.

c. The electronic economy

- The 'electronic economy' is another factor that underpins economic globalisation.
- Banks, corporations, fund managers and individual investors are able to shift funds internationally with the click of a mouse.
- This new ability to move 'electronic money' instantaneously carries it with great risks however.
- In India often this is discussed with reference to rising stock markets and also sudden dips because of foreign investors buying stocks, making a profit and then selling them off.

d. The Weightless economy or knowledge economy

- The weightless economy is one in which products have their base in information, as in the case with computer software, media and entertainment products and internetbased services.
- A knowledge economy is one in which much of the workforce is involved not in the physical production or distribution of material goods, but in their design, development, technology, marketing, sale and servicing.
- It can range from the neighbourhood catering service to large organisations involved in providing a host of services for both professional meets like conferences to family events like weddings.

e. Globalisation of finance

- For the first time, mainly due to the information technology revolution, there has been a globalisation of finance.
- Globally integrated financial markets undertake billions of dollars worth transactions within seconds in the electronic circuits.
- There is a 24-hour trading in capital and security markets. Cities such as New York, Tokyo and London are the key centers for financial trading. Within India, Mumbai is known as the financial capital of the country.

• Global Communications

- Important advances in technology and the world's telecommunications infrastructure has led to revolutionary changes in global communication.
- Some homes and many offices now have multiple links to the outside world, including telephones (land lines and mobiles), fax machines, digital and cable television, electronic mail and the internet.
- Despite this digital divide these forms of technology do facilitate the 'compression' of time and space.
- The process of globalisation is giving rise to network and media society.
- To create global interconnectedness more efficiently, the Government of India has initiated an ambitious programme in the form of 'Digital India', in which every exchange will incorporate digitisation.
- It will transform India into a 'digitally empowered society and a 'knowledge economy'.

- Cellular telephony has also grown enormously and cell phones are a part of the self for most urban-based middle class youth. There has been a tremendous growth in the usage of cell phones and a marked change in how its use is seen.

• Globalisation And Labour

- A new international division of labour has emerged in which more and more routine manufacturing production and employment is done in the Third World cities.

> Nike grew enormously from its inception in the 1960s. Nike grew as an importer of shoes. The founder Phil Knight imported shoes from Japan and sold them at athletics meetings. The company grew to a multinational enterprise, a transnational corporation. Its headquarters are in Beverton, just outside Portland, Oregon. Only two US factories ever made shoes for Nike. In the 1960s they were made in Japan. As costs increased production shifted to South Korea in mid-1970s. **Labour costs grew in South Korea, so in the 1980s production widened to Thailand and Indonesia**. Since the 1990s we in India produce Nike. **However, if labour is cheaper elsewhere production centres will move somewhere else. This entire process makes the labouring population very vulnerable and insecure**. This flexibility of labour often works in favour of the producers. Instead of mass production of goods at a centralised location (Fordism), we have moved to a system of flexible production at dispersed locations (post-Fordism).

• Globalisation And Employment

- Another key issue regarding globalisation and labour is the relationship between employment and globalisation.
- For the middle class youth from urban centers, globalisation and the IT revolution has opened up new career opportunities.
- Instead of routinely picking up BSc/BA/BCom degree from colleges, many young persons are learning computer languages at computer institutes, taking up jobs at call centers or Business Process Outsourcing (BPO) companies, working as sales persons in shopping malls or picking up jobs at the various restaurants that have opened up.

- **Globalisation And Political Changes**
  - In many ways it was a major political change, namely, the collapse of the erstwhile socialist world that hastened globalisation.
  - And also gave a specific economic and political approach to the economic policies that underpin globalisation. These changes are often termed as neo-liberal economic measures.
  - Broadly these policies reflect a political vision of free enterprise which believes that a free reign to market forces will be both efficient and fair. It is, therefore, critical of both state regulation and state subsidies.
  - The existing process of globalisation in this sense does have a political vision as much as an economic vision.
  - We, have the concept of an inclusive globalisation, that is one, which includes all sections of society.
  - Another significant political development which is accompanying globalisation is the growth of international and regional mechanisms for political collaboration.
  - The European Union (EU), the Association of South East Asian Nations (ASEAN), South Asian Association for Regional Corporation (SAARC) are just some of the examples that indicate the greater role of regional associations.
  - The other political dimension has been the rise of International Governmental Organisations. (IGOs) and International Non-Governmental Organisations (INGOs).
  - An intergovernmental organisation is a body that is established by participating governments and given responsibility for regulating, or overseeing a particular domain of activity that is transnational in scope.
  - The World Trade Organisation (WTO) for instance increasingly has a major say in the rules that govern trade practices.
  - INGOs differ from intergovernmental organisations in that they are not affiliated with government institutions.
  - Rather they are independent organisations, which make policy decisions and address international issues.
  - Some of the best known INGOs are Greenpeace (see chapter 8), The Red Cross, Amnesty International and Medecins Sans Frontieres (Doctors Without Borders).

- **Globalisation And Culture**
  - There are many ways that globalisation affects culture.
  - Thus there are heated debates in our society not just about political and economic issues but also about changes in clothes, styles, music, films, languages, body language.
  - A central contention is that all cultures will become similar, that is homogeneous.
  - Glocalisation refers to the mixing of the global with the local. It is not entirely spontaneous. Nor is it entirely delinked from the commercial interests of globalization.
  - It is a strategy often adopted by foreign firms while dealing with local traditions in order to enhance their marketability.
  - In India, we find that all the foreign television channels like Star, MTV, Channel V and Cartoon Network use Indian languages.
  - Even McDonald's sells only vegetarian and chicken products in India and not its beef products, which are popular abroad. McDonald's goes vegetarian during the Navaratri festival. In the field of music, one can see the growth of popularity of 'Bhangra pop', 'Indi pop', fusion music and even remixes.

- **Gender And Culture**
  - Globalisation can be taken as a bogey to defend unjust practices against women.
  - Fortunately for us in India we have been able to retain and develop a democratic tradition and culture that allows us to define culture in a more inclusive and democratic fashion.

- **Culture Of Consumption**
  - Till the 1970s the manufacturing industries used to play a major role in the growth of cities. Presently, cultural consumption (of art, food, fashion, music, tourism) shapes to a large extent the growth of cities.
  - This is evident in the spurt in the growth of shopping malls, multiplex cinema halls, amusement parks and 'water world' in every major city in India.
  - Most significantly advertisements and the media in general promote a culture where spending is important.

- **Corporate Culture**
  - Corporate culture is a branch of management theory that seeks to increase productivity and competitiveness though the creation of a unique

organisational culture involving all members of a firm.

- A dynamic corporate culture - involving company events, rituals and traditions - is thought to enhance employee loyalty and promote group solidarity. It also refers to way of doing things, of promotion and packaging products.

- The spread of multinational companies and the opportunities opened up by the information technology revolution has created in the metropolitan cities in India class of upwardly mobile professionals working in software companies, multinational banks, chartered accountancy firms, stock markets, travel, fashion designing, entertainment, media and other allied fields.

- These high-flying professionals have highly stressful work schedules, get exorbitant salaries and are the main clientele of the booming consumer industry.

Exercise

1. Some years back, there were reports of large number of suicides by the traditional weavers in Sircilla village of Karimnagar district and in Dubakka village in Medak district, both in Andhra Pradesh. The reason of suicide attempts was -
(a) No money to invest in technology
(b) Boom in the powerloom sector
(c) Increase in the market competition
(d) All of the above

2. Which of the following is true about corporate culture?
(a) It seeks to increase productivity and competitiveness
(b) Company events, rituals and traditions enhances its profit.
(c) It keep on engaging employees through periodical amusements.
(d) None of the above

3. The examples of cultural consumption are -
(a) Street market   (b) Multiplex cinema
(c) Open theatres   (d) Cultural theatres

4. McDonald's goes vegetarian during the Navaratri festival, is an example of -
(a) Globalization   (b) Marketization
(c) Glocalization   (d) Commoditification

5. India is member of which of the following regional organizations?
I. European Union
II. ASEAN
III. SAARC
(a) I and II   (b) II and III
(c) I and III   (d) All of the above

6. World Trade Organization is an example of the following -
(a) International governmental organization
(b) Inter-governmental organization
(c) International non-governmental organization
(d) Regional organization

7. Which of the following changes hastened globalization?
I. Collapse of socialist world
II. Specific economic and political approach to the economic policies
(a) I only   (b) II only
(c) Both I and II   (d) Neither I nor II

Read the following passage and answer the following questions 8, 9 and 10

The condition of our dombari community is very bad. Television and radio have snatched away our means of livelihood. We perform acrobatics but because of the circus and the television, which have reached even in remote corners and villages, nobody is interested in our performances. We do not get even a pittance, however hard we perform. People watch our shows but just for entertainment, they never pay us anything. They never bother about the fact that we are hungry. Our profession is dying.

8. Dombari community's condition is degrading due to -
(a) Loss of people's attention
(b) Radio and television presents the same performance easily
(c) Decline of circus culture
(d) None of the above

9. Acrobatics performance by Dombari community is no more interesting among the people. The reason is -
   (a) Circus and television has made it reach to the remotest areas
   (b) Easy availability of performance
   (c) The culture of acrobatics is dying
   (d) All of the above

10. The central problem among dombari community is -
    (a) Decline of culture (b) Uninterested crowd
    (c) Globalization   (d) None of the above

11. Which of the following is true about the concept of an inclusive globalization?
    (a) Representation of all the sections of society
    (b) Inclusion of all the section of society
    (c) Inclusion of downtrodden section
    (d) Reaching to the rural areas

12. The largest number of poor people lives in South Asia. Particularly the poverty rate is high in which of the following South Asian countries?
    I.   India   II. China
    III. Nepal   IV. Bangladesh
    (a) I, II and III   (b) II, III and IV
    (c) I, III and IV   (d) All of the above

13. In case of Nike shoe company, shift of production took place due to increase in the labor cost. This phenomenon leads to -
    (a) Loss of revenue to the government
    (b) Make labor population very vulnerable and insecure
    (c) Reduction in the foreign exchange
    (d) Increase in the poverty

14. Rural areas are still unconnected through internet. What are the possible reasons?
    I.   Illiteracy
    II. Lack of infrastructure
    III. Lack of government funding
    IV. Erratic power supply
    (a) I, II and IV   (b) II, III and IV
    (c) I, II and III   (d) All of the above

15. **Assertion (A):** Globally integrated financial markets undertake billions of dollars worth transactions within seconds in the electronic circuits.

    Reason (R): For the first time, mainly due to the information technology revolution, there has been a globalisation of finance.

    (a) Both A and R are true and R is the correct explanation of A
    (b) Both A and R are true and R is not the correct explanation of A
    (c) A is true and R is false
    (d) A is false and R is true

16. Which of the following cities are known as financial trading cities?
    I.   New York
    II. Delhi
    III. Mumbai
    (a) I and II   (b) I and III
    (c) II and III   (d) All of the above

17. An economy in which workforce is not involved in the physical production, is known as
    (a) Organized sector
    (b) Unorganized sector
    (c) Knowledge economy
    (d) Electronic economy

18. Banks, corporations, fund managers and individual investors are part of which type of economy?
    (a) Physical economy
    (b) Knowledge economy
    (c) Virtual economy
    (d) Electronic economy

19. Which of the following statements are correct regarding transnational companies?
    I.   They produce goods or market services in more than one country.
    II. They are relatively big firms with their factories outside the country in which they are based.
    III. They could also be gigantic international ones whose operations criss-cross the globe.
    (a) I and II
    (b) II and III
    (c) I and III
    (d) All of the above

20. Due to liberalization, India economy witnessed reforms in the following sectors -
    I.   Agriculture
    II. Foreign investment
    III. Financial investment
    (a) I and II
    (b) II and III
    (c) III only
    (d) All of the above

Answer Keys

1. (d)	2. (a)	3. (b)	4. (c)	5. (b)	6. (a)	7. (c)	8. (b)	9. (a)	10. (c)
11. (b)	12. (c)	13. (b)	14. (a)	15. (a)	16. (b)	17. (c)	18. (d)	19. (c)	20. (d)

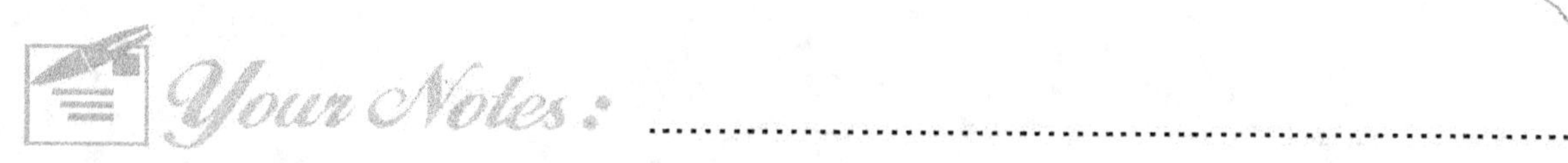
Your Notes :

CHAPTER 7

Mass Media and Communication

Chapter at Glance

- A wide variety of forms, including television, newspapers, films, magazines, radio, advertisements, video games and CDs are referred to as 'mass' media because they reach mass audiences.
- It is obvious that there has been a phenomenal expansion of mass communication of all kinds in recent years.
- There are many aspects to this growth which is of great interest to us -
  i. While we recognise the specificity of the current communication revolution, it is important to go back a little and sketch out the growth of modern mass media in the world and in India.
     - This helps us realise that like any other social institution the structure and content of mass media is shaped by changes in the economic, political and socio-cultural contexts.
     - For instance, we see how central the state and its vision of development influenced the media in the first decades after independence. And how in the post 1990 period of globalisation the market has a key role to play.
  ii. This help us better appreciate how the relationship between mass media and communication with society is dialectical. Both influence each other.
     - The nature and role of mass media is influenced by the society in which it is located. At the same time the far reaching influence of mass media on society cannot be over-emphasised.
  iii. Mass communication is different from other means of communication as it requires a formal structural organisation to meet large-scale capital, production and management demands.
  iv. There are sharp differences between how easily different sections of people can use mass media.

The Beginnings Of Modern Mass Media

- The first modern mass media institution began with the development of the printing press.
- The first attempts at printing books using modern technologies began in Europe.
- This technique was first developed by Johann Gutenberg in 1440. Initial attempts at printing were restricted to religious books.
- With the Industrial Revolution, the print industry also grew.
- The first products of the press were restricted to an audience of literate elites.
- It was only in the mid 19th century, with further development in technologies, transportation and literacy that newspapers began to reach out to a mass audience.
- It made people feel connected and develop a sense of belonging or 'we feeling'.
- Scholar Benedict Anderson has thus argued that this helped the growth of nationalism, the feeling that people who did not even know of each other's existence feel like members of a family.
- Anderson thus suggested that we could think of the nation as an 'imagined community'

Nationalism and Press in India

- The growth of Indian nationalism was closely linked to its struggle against colonialism. It emerged in the wake of the institutional changes brought about by British rule in India.
- Anti-colonial public opinion was nurtured and channelised by the nationalist press, which was

vocal in its opposition to the oppressive measures of the colonial state.

- This led the colonial government to clamp down on the nationalist press and impose censorship, for instance during the Ilbert Bill agitation in 1883.

- Association with the national movement led some of the nationalist newspapers like Kesari (Marathi), Mathrubhumi (Malayalam), Amrita Bazar Patrika (English) to suffer the displeasure of the colonial state.

- But that did not prevent them from advocating the nationalist cause and demand an end to colonial rule.

- Under British rule newspapers and magazines, films and radio comprised the range of mass media.

- Radio was wholly owned by the state. National views could not be, therefore, expressed. Newspapers and films though autonomous from the state were strictly monitored by the Raj.

- Newspapers and magazines either in English or vernacular were not very widely circulated as the literate public was limited.

- The print media carried a range of opinion, which expressed their ideas of a 'free India'. These variations were carried over to independent India.

Mass Media In Independent India

- In independent India, the first Prime Minister Jawaharlal Nehru, called upon the media to function as the watchdog of democracy.

- The media was expected to spread the spirit of self-reliance and national development among the people.

- The media was seen as a means to inform the people of the various developmental efforts.

- The media was also encouraged to fight against oppressive social practices like untouchability, child marriages, and ostracism of widows, as well as beliefs of witchcraft and faith healing.

- A rational, scientific ethos was to be promoted for the building of a modern industrial society.

- The Films Division of the government produced newsreels and documentaries.

- These were shown before the screening of films in every movie theatre, documenting the development process as directed by the state

Radio

- Radio broadcasting which commenced in India through amateur 'ham' broadcasting clubs in Kolkata and Chennai in the 1920s matured into a public broadcasting system in the 1940s during the World War II when it became a major instrument of propaganda for Allied forces in South-east Asia.

- At the time of independence there were only 6 radio stations located in the major cities catering primarily to an urban audience. By 1950 there were 5,46,200 radio licences all over India.

- Since the media was seen as an active partner in the development of the newly free nation, the AIR's programmes consisted mainly of news, current affairs, discussions on development.

- Apart from All India Radio (AIR) broadcasts news there was Vividh Bharati, a channel for entertainment that was primarily broadcasting Hindi film songs on listeners' request.

- In 1957 AIR acquired the hugely popular channel Vividh Bharati, which soon began to carry sponsored programmes and advertisements and grew to become a money-spinning channel for AIR.

- When India gained independence in 1947, All India Radio had an infrastructure of six radio stations, located in metropolitan cities.

- After independence the government gave priority to the expansion of the radio broadcasting infrastructure, especially in state capitals and in border areas.

- Over the years, AIR has developed a formidable infrastructure for radio broadcasting in India. It operates a three-tiered - national, regional, and local - service to cater to India's geographic, linguistic and cultural diversity.

- The major constraint for the popularisation of radio initially was the cost of the radio set.

- The transistor revolution in the 1960s made the radio more accessible by making it mobile as battery operated sets and reducing the unit price substantially.

- In 2000, around 110 million households (two-thirds of all Indian households) were listening to radio broadcasts in 24 languages and 146 dialects.

- More than a third of them were rural households.

- As of today, the AIR has grown to 480 stations and 681 transmitters covering 99% of the population spread over 92% area of the country.

Television

- Television programming was introduced experimentally in India to promote rural development as early as 1959.

- Later, the Satellite Instructional Television Experiment (SITE) broadcasted directly to community viewers in the rural areas of six states between August 1975 and July 1976.

- Meanwhile, television stations were set up under Doordarshan in four cities (Delhi, Mumbai, Srinagar and Amritsar) by 1975.
- Three more stations in Kolkata, Chennai and Jalandhar were added within a year.
- Every broadcasting centre had its own mix of programmes, comprising news, children's and women's programmes, farmers' programmes, as well as, entertainment programmes.
- The advent of colour broadcasting during the 1982 Asian Games in Delhi and the rapid expansion of the national network led to rapid commercialisation of television broadcasting.
- During 1984-85 the number of television transmitters increased all over India, covering a large proportion of the population.
- It was also the time when indigenous soap operas, like Hum Log (1984-85) and Buniyaad (1986- 87) were aired.
- They were hugely popular and attracted substantial advertising revenue for Doordarshan as did the broadcasting of the epics-Ramayana (1987-88) and Mahabharata (1988-90).
- Today, the Annual Report released by TRAI for the year 2015-16 clearly stated that India has the world's second largest TV market after China.

Print Media

- The beginnings of the print media and its role in both the spread of the social reform movement and the nationalist movement have been noted.
- After Independence, the print media continued to share the general approach of being a partner in the task of nation building by taking up developmental issues, as well as, giving voice to the widest section of people.
- The gravest challenge that the media faced was with the declaration of Emergency in 1975 and censorship of the media. Fortunately, the period ended and democracy was restored in 1977. India with its many problems can be justifiably proud of a free media.

Globalisation And The Media

- The media have always had international dimensions - such as the gathering of new stories and the distribution of primarily western films overseas.
- The media industry was also differentiated into distinct sectors - for the most part, cinema, print media, radio and television broadcasting all operated independently of one another.

The changes that globalisation has brought about on the print media (primarily newspapers and magazines), the electronic media (primarily television), and on the radio.

Print Media

- In India, we have seen the circulation of newspapers grow.
- New technologies have helped boost the production and circulation of newspapers. A large number of glossy magazines have also made their entry to the market.
- As is evident, the reasons for this amazing growth in Indian language newspapers are many.
  - i. First, there is a rise in the number of literate people who are migrating to cities.
  - ii. Second, the needs of the readers in the small towns and villages are different from that of the cities and the Indian language newspapers cater to those needs.
- Dominant Indian language newspapers such as Malayala Manorama and the Eenadu launched the concept of local news in a significant manner by introducing district and whenever necessary, block editions.
- Dina Thanthi, another leading Tamil newspaper, has always used simplified and colloquial language.
- Marketing strategies have also marked the Dainik Bhaskar group's growth as they carry out consumer contact programmes, door-to-door surveys, and research.
- While English newspapers, often called 'national dailies', circulate across regions, vernacular newspapers have vastly increased their circulation in the states and the rural hinterland.
- In order to compete with the electronic media, newspapers, especially English language newspapers have on the one hand reduced prices and on the other hand brought out editions from multiple centres.

Television

- While Doordarshan was expanding rapidly in the 1980s, the cable television industry was mushrooming in major Indian cities.
- The VCR greatly multiplied entertainment options for Indian audiences, providing alternatives to Doordarshan's single channel programming.
- The coming in of transnational television companies like Star TV, MTV, Channel [V], Sony and others, worried some people on the likely impact on Indian youth and on the Indian cultural identity.

- The early strategy of Sony International was to broadcast 10 Hindi films a week, gradually decreasing the number as the station produced its own Hindi language content.

- The majority of the foreign networks have now introduced either a segment of Hindi language programming (MTV India), or an entire new Hindi language channel (STAR Plus).

- STAR Sports and ESPN have dual commentary or an audio sound track in Hindi. The larger players have launched specific regional channels in languages such as Bengali, Punjabi, Marathi and Gujarati.

- Most television channels are on throughout the day, 24X7.

- Television has fostered public debate and is expanding its reach every passing year.

Radio

- In 2000, AIR's programmes could be heard in two-third of all Indian households in 24 languages and 146 dialects, over some 120 million radio sets.

- The advent of privately owned FM radio stations in 2002 provided a boost to entertainment programmes

- over radio. In order to attract audiences these privately run radio stations sought to provide entertainment to its listeners.

- As privately run FM channels are not permitted to broadcast any political news bulletins, many of these channel specialise in 'particular kinds' of popular music to retain their audiences.

- Most of the FM channels which are popular among young urban professionals and students, often belong to media conglomerates. Like 'Radio Mirchi' belongs to the Times of India group, Red FM is owned by Living Media and Radio City by the Star Network.

- But independent radio stations engaged in public broadcastings like National Public Radio (USA) or BBC (UK) are missing from our broadcasting landscape.

- Further privatisation of radio stations and the emergence of community owned radio stations would lead to the growth of radio stations.

- The demand for local news is growing. The number of homes listening to FM in India has also reinforced the world wide trend of networks getting replaced by local radio

Exercise

1. Which of the following are forms of mass media?
   I.   CDs
   II. Advertisements
   III. Video games
   (a) I only   (b) II and III
   (c) I and II   (d) All of the above

2. Choose the correct statements regarding mass media:
   I.   Mass media is shaped by changes in the economic, political and socio-cultural contexts.
   II. The nature and role of mass media is influenced by the society in which it is located.
   (a) I only
   (b) II only
   (c) Both I and II
   (d) Neither I nor II

3. The first attempts at printing books using modern technologies started in -
   (a) United States of America
   (b) Europe
   (c) Germany
   (d) France

4. Printing press was first discovered by ______________ and initially it was restricted to print ______________ .
   (a) Johann Gutenberg, religious books
   (b) Johann Gutenberg, Newspapers
   (c) Benedict Anderson, Political news
   (d) None of the above

5. Which of the following statements are correct regarding printing press?
   I.   Printing press grew with the growth of Industrial Revolution.
   II. The first products of the press were restricted to an audience of literate elites.
   III. In the mid-19th century, with further development in technologies, transportation and literacy, newspapers reached out to a mass audience.
   (a) I and II   (b) II and III
   (c) I and III   (d) All of the above

6. 'Imagined community' was suggested by Benedict Anderson in the context of -
   (a) Nationality   (b) Nation
   (c) People   (d) Castes

7. Ilbert Bill Agitation had been organized in India in the following year -
   (a) 1773 (b) 1793
   (c) 1883 (d) 1905

8. Mathrubhumi was a nationalist newspaper which used to be published in the following language:
   (a) English (b) Hindi
   (c) Marathi (d) Malayalam

9. Sambad Kaumudi and Mirat-ul-Akhbar was started by which of the following personality?
   (a) Bankimchandra Chatterjee
   (b) Raja Rammohun Roy
   (c) Ishwarchand Vidyasagar
   (d) M G Ranade

10. Bombay Samachar was started by ………………………………… in the language …………………………
   (a) Fardoonji Murzban, Gujarati
   (b) Dadabhai Naoroji, Marathi
   (c) Raja Rammohun Roy, English
   (d) B G Tilak, Marathi

11. Which of the following is true regarding mass media in independent India?
   I. It meant to inform the people of the various developmental efforts.
   II. It encouraged fight against oppressive social practices like untouchability, child marriage, etc.
   III. A rational, scientific ethos was to be promoted for the building of a modern industrial society.
   (a) II and III (b) III only
   (c) I and II (d) All of the above

12. A major countryside campaign on hybrid crops on a sustained day-to-day basis for over 10 years from 1967 was undertaken by the following?
   (a) Vividh Bharti (b) All India Radio
   (c) Doordarshan (d) Newspaper

13. The three tier operation of All India Radio was catered to the following -
   I. Geographic diversity
   II. Linguistic diversity
   III. Cultural diversity
   (a) I and II (b) II and III
   (c) I and III (d) All of the above

14. SITE was used to reach to the rural area in the field of -
   (a) Television (b) Radio
   (c) Newspaper (d) Mobile

15. What position India holds in the TV market as per the Annual Report released by TRAI in 2015-16?
   (a) First (b) Second
   (c) Third (d) Fourth

16. A large number of glossy magazines have also made their entry to the market. This change took place due to
   (a) Privatization of media
   (b) Competitiveness in the market
   (c) Globalization in the media
   (d) None of the above

17. The Eenadu story also exemplifies the success of the Indian language press. Who was the founder of Eenadu?
   (a) Ramoji Rao (b) Baji Rao
   (c) B G Tilak (d) P Sriramalu

18. Malayala Manorama and Dina Thanthi are examples of -
   (a) National Newspapers
   (b) Regional news channels
   (c) Local language newspapers
   (d) Regional radio stations

19. National Public Radio belongs to which of the following country?
   (a) United Kingdom
   (b) United States of America
   (c) China
   (d) West Asia

20. **Assertion (A):** Further privatisation of radio stations and the emergence of community owned radio stations would lead to the growth of radio stations.
   Reason (R): The potential for using FM channels is enormous and number of homes listening to FM is increasing.
   (a) Both A and R are true and R is the correct explanation of A
   (b) Both A and R are true and R is not the correct explanation of A
   (c) A is true and R is false
   (d) A is false and R is true

Answer Keys

1. (d)	2. (c)	3. (b)	4. (a)	5. (d)	6. (b)	7. (c)	8. (d)	9. (b)	10. (a)
11. (d)	12. (b)	13. (d)	14. (a)	15. (b)	16. (c)	17. (a)	18. (c)	19. (b)	20. (b)

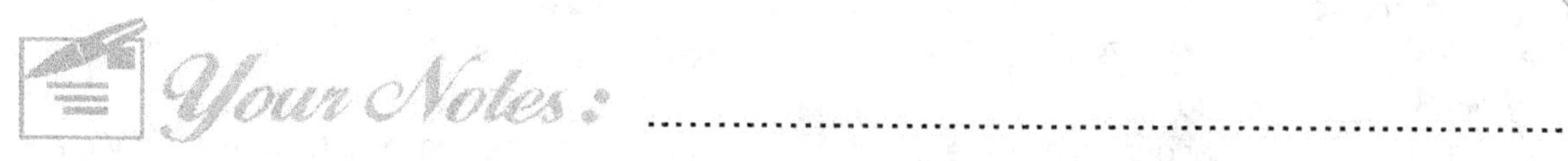
Your Notes :

CHAPTER 8

Social Movements

Chapter at Glance

- Social movements have shaped the world we live in and continue to do so.

- The socialist movements world over, the civil rights movement in the United States in the 1950s and 1960s that fought for equal rights for Blacks, the anti-apartheid struggle in South Africa have all changed the world in fundamental ways.

- Social movements not only change societies; they also inspire other social movements.

Features Of A Social Movement

- A social movement requires sustained collective action over time. Such action is often directed against the state and takes the form of demanding changes in state policy or practice. Spontaneous, disorganised protest cannot be called a social movement either.

- Collective action must be marked by some degree of organisation.

- This organisation may include a leadership and a structure that defines how members relate to each other, make decisions and carry them out.

- Those participating in a social movement also have shared objectives and ideologies.

- A social movement has a general orientation or way of approaching to bring about (or to prevent) change.

- These defining features are not constant. They may change over the course of a social movement's life.

- Social movements often arise with the aim of bringing about changes on a public issue, such as ensuring the right of the tribal population to use the forests or the right of displaced people to settlement and compensation.

- While social movements seek to bring in social change, counter movements sometimes arise in defence of status quo.

- There are many instances of such counter movements.

- When Raja Rammohun Roy campaigned against sati and formed the Brahmo Samaj, defenders of sati formed Dharma Sabha and petitioned the British not to legislate against sati.

- When reformers demanded education for girls, many protested that this would be disastrous for society.

- When reformers campaigned for widow remarriage, they were socially boycotted. When the so called 'lower caste' children enrolled in schools, some so called 'upper caste' children were withdrawn from the schools by their families.

- Peasant movements have often been brutally suppressed. More recently the social movements of erstwhile excluded groups like the Dalits have often invoked retaliatory action.

- Social movement activists hold meetings to mobilise people around the issues that concern them.

- Such activities help shared understanding, and also prepare for a feeling of agreement or consensus about how to pursue the collective agenda.

- Social movements also chart out campaigns that include lobbying with the government, media and other important makers of public opinion.

- Gandhi adopted novel ways such as ahimsa, satyagraha and his use of the charkha in the freedom movement.

Distinguishing Social Change And Social Movements

- Social change is continuous and ongoing.

- The broad historical processes of social change are the sum total of countless individual and collective actions gathered across time and space.

- Social movements are directed towards some specific goals. It involves long and continuous social effort and action by people.

Sociology And Social Movements

Why The Study Of Social Movements Is Important For Sociology

- From the very beginning, the discipline of sociology has been interested in social movements.

- The French Revolution was the violent culmination of several movements aimed at overthrowing the monarchy and establishing 'liberty, equality and fraternity'.

- In Britain, the industrial revolution was marked by great social upheaval.

- Poor labourers and artisans who had left the countryside to find work in the cities protested against the inhuman living conditions into which they were forced.

- Food riots in England were often suppressed by the government.

- Scholars influenced by the ideas of Karl Marx offered a different view of violent collective action. Historians like E. P. Thompson showed that the 'crowd' and the 'mob' were not made up of anarchic hooligans out to destroy society. Instead, they too had a 'moral economy'.

Theories Of Social Movements

- According to the theory of relative deprivation, social conflict arises when a social group feels that it is worse off than others around it. Such conflict is likely to result in successful collective protest.

  - This theory emphasises the role of psychological factors such as resentment and rage in inciting social movements.

  - The limitations of this theory are that while perceptions of deprivation may be a necessary condition for collective action, they are not a sufficient reason in themselves.

- Mancur Olson's book The Logic of Collective Action argues that a social movement is an aggregation of rational individual actors pursuing their self-interest.

  - A person will join a social movement only if s/he will gain something from it. S/he will participate only if the risks are less than the gains.

  - Olson's theory is based on the notion of the rational, utility-maximising individual.

- McCarthy and Zald's proposed resource mobilisation theory rejected Olson's assumption that social movements are made up of individuals pursuing their self-interest.

  - Instead, they argued that a social movement's success depends on its ability to mobilise resources or means of different sorts.

  - If a movement can muster resources such as leadership, organisational capacity, and communication facilities, and can use them within the available political opportunity structure, it is more likely to be effective.

  - It can create resources such as new symbols and identities. As numerous poor people's movements show, scarcity of resources need not be a constraint.

Types Of Social Movements

One Way Of Classifying: Reformist, Redemptive, Revolutionary

- There are different kinds of social movements. They can be classified as: (i) redemptive or transformatory; (ii) reformist; and (iii) revolutionary.

- A redemptive social movement aims to bring about a change in the personal consciousness and actions of its individual members. For instance, people in the Ezhava community in Kerala were led by Narayana Guru to change their social practices.

- Reformist social movements strive to change the existing social and political arrangements through gradual, incremental steps.

  - The 1960s movement for the reorganisation of Indian states on the basis of language and the recent Right to Information campaign are examples of reformist movements.

- Revolutionary social movements attempt to radically transform social relations, often by capturing state power.

  - The Bolshevik revolution in Russia that deposed the Tsar to create a communist state and the Naxalite movement in India that seeks to remove oppressive landlords and state officials can be described as revolutionary movements.

Interpretation of Social Movement

- It differs from one section to another.

- For instance, what was a 'mutiny' or 'rebellion' for British colonial rulers in 1857 was 'the first war of Independence' for Indian nationalists.

- A mutiny is an act of defiance against supposedly legitimate authority, i.e., the British rule.

- A struggle for independence is a challenge to the very legitimacy of British rule.

- This shows how people attach different meanings to social movements.

Another Way Of Classifying: Old And New

- Most of the twentieth century social movements were class based such as working class movements and peasant movements or anti-colonial movements.

- While anti-colonial movements united entire people into national liberation struggles, class-based movements united classes to fight for their rights.
- The most far-reaching social movements of the last century thus have been class-based or based on national liberation struggles.
- Besides bringing about the formation of communist and socialist states across the world, most notably in the Soviet Union, China, and Cuba, these movements also led to the reform of capitalism.
- The creation of welfare states that protected workers' rights and offered universal education, health care and social security in the capitalist nations of Western Europe was partly due to political pressure created by the communist and socialist movements.
- The movement against colonialism has been as influential as the movement against capitalism. Since capitalism and colonialism have usually been interlinked through forms of imperialism, social movements have simultaneously targeted both these forms of exploitation.
- That is, nationalist movements have mobilised against rule by a foreign power as well as against the dominance of foreign capital.
- The decades after the Second World War witnessed the end of empire and the formation of new nation-states as a result of nationalist movements in India, Egypt, Indonesia, and many other countries.
- Since then, another wave of social movements occurred in the 1960s and early 1970s.
- This was the time of the war in Vietnam where forces led by the United States of America were involved in a bloody conflict in the former French colony against Communist guerrillas.
- In Europe, Paris was the nucleus of a vibrant students' movement that joined workers' parties in a series of strikes protesting against the war.
- Across the Atlantic, the United States of America was experiencing a surge of social protest.
- The civil rights movement led by Martin Luther King had been followed by the Black Power movement led by Malcolm X.
- The anti-war movement was joined by tens of thousands of students who were being compulsorily drafted by the government to go and fight in Vietnam.
- The women's movement and the environmental movement also gained strength during this time of social ferment.
- It was difficult to classify the members of these so-called 'new social movements' as belonging to the same class or even nation.

Distinguishing The New Social Movement From The Old Social Movements

I. Different historical context

- That was a period when nationalist movements were overthrowing colonial powers.
- The working class movements in the capitalist west were wresting better wages, better living conditions, social security, free schooling and health security from the state.
- That was also a period when socialist movements were establishing new kinds of states and societies.
- The old social movements clearly saw reorganisation of power relations as a central goal.

II. Framing of political parties

- The old social movements functioned within the frame of political parties. The Indian National Congress led the Indian National Movement. The Communist Party of China led the Chinese Revolution.
- So the 'new' social movements were not about changing the distribution of power in society but about quality-of-life issues such as having a clean environment.

III. Role of political parties

- In the old social movements, the role of political parties was central.
- People left out by the formal political system join social movements or non-party political formations in order to put pressure on the state from outside.
- Today, the broader term of civil society is used to refer to both old social movements represented by political parties and trade unions and to new nongovernmental organisations, women's groups, environmental groups and tribal activists.

IV. Scope of movement

- The various dimensions of social change in India you would have been struck by the fact that globalisation has been re-shaping peoples' lives in industry and agriculture, culture and media.
- Often legal arrangements that are binding are international such as the regulations of the World Trade Organisation (WTO).
- Environmental and health risks, fears of nuclear warfare are global in nature. Not surprisingly therefore many of the new social movements are international in scope.

India's Case

- India has experienced a whole array of social movements involving women, peasants, Dalits, Adivasis, and others.
- Peasant movements have mobilised for better prices for their produce and protested against the removal of agricultural subsidies.
- Dalit labourers have acted collectively to ensure that they are not exploited by upper-caste landowners and moneylenders.
- The women's movement has worked on issues of gender discrimination in diverse spheres like the workplace and within the family.
- At the same time, these new social movements are not just about 'old' issues of economic inequality.
- Nor are they organised along class lines alone. Identity politics, cultural anxieties and aspirations are essential elements in creating social movements and occur in ways that are difficult to trace to class-based inequality.
- For instance, the women's movement includes urban, middle-class feminists as well as poor peasant women.
- The regional movements for separate statehood bring together different groups of people who do not share homogeneous class identities.
- In a social movement, questions of social inequality can occur alongside other, equally important, issues.

Ecological Movements

- Over the decades there has been a great deal of concern about the unchecked use of natural resources and a model of development that creates new needs that further demands greater exploitation of the already depleted natural resources.
- This model of development has also been critiqued for assuming that all sections of people will be beneficiaries of development.
- The impact of industrial pollution is yet another story.
- The Chipko Movement, an example of the ecological movement, in the Himalayan foothills is a good example of such intermingled interests and ideologies.
- According to Ramachandra Guha in his book, Unquiet Woods, villagers rallied together to save the oak and rhododendron forests near their villages.
- When government forest contractors came to cut down the trees, villagers, including large number of women, stepped forward to hug the trees to prevent their being felled.
- All of them relied on the forest to get firewood, fodder and other daily necessities.
- This conflict placed the livelihood needs of poor villagers against the government's desire to generate revenues from selling timber.
- The economy of subsistence was pitted against the economy of profit.
- Along with this issue of social inequality (villagers versus a government that represented commercial, capitalist interests), the Chipko Movement also raised the issue of ecological sustainability.
- Cutting down natural forests was a form of environmental destruction that had resulted in devastating floods and landslides in the region.
- For the villagers, these 'red' and 'green' issues were interlinked. While their survival depended on the survival of the forest, they also valued the forest for its own sake as a form of ecological wealth that benefits all.
- The Chipko Movement also expressed the resentment of hill villagers against a distant government headquartered in the plains that seemed indifferent and hostile to their concerns.
- So, concerns about economy, ecology and political representation underlay the Chipko Movement.
- Trees are necessary for the conservation of environment.
- Similarly, clean water is necessary for a healthy environment. In the light of this, the Government of India has recently, through the 'Integrated Ganga Conservation Mission' (Namami Gange) and Swachch Bharat Abhiyan imitated systematic efforts to create a balance, structure and quality in India's ecology.

Class Based Movements

Peasant Movements

- Peasant movements or agrarian struggles have taken place from pre-colonial days. The movements in the period between 1858 and 1914 tended to remain localised, disjointed and confined to particular grievances.
- Bengal revolt of 1859-62 against the indigo plantation system and the 'Deccan riots' of 1857 against moneylenders.
- Later on under the leadership of Mahatma Gandhi it partially linked to the Independence movement.
- Bardoli Satyagraha (1928, Surat District) a 'non-tax' campaign as part of the nationwide non-cooperation movement, a campaign of refusal to

- pay land revenue and the Champaran Satyagraha (1917-18) directed against indigo plantations.
- In the 1920s, protest movements against the forest policies of the British government and local rulers arose in certain regions.

Between 1920 and 1940 Peasant Organisations Arose

- The first organisation to be founded was the Bihar Provincial Kisan Sabha (1929) and in 1936 the All India Kisan Sabha.
- The peasants organised by the Sabhas demanded freedom from economic exploitation for peasants, workers and all other exploited classes.
- At the time of Independence we had the two most classical cases of peasant movements, namely the Tebhaga movement (1946-7) and the Telangana movement (1946-51).
- The first was a struggle of sharecroppers in Bengal in North Bihar for two thirds share of their produce instead of the customary half.
- It had the support of the Kisan Sabha and the Communist Party of India (CPI).
- The second, directed against the feudal conditions in the princely state of Hyderabad and was led by the CPI.
- Certain issues which had dominated colonial times changed after independence.
- For land reforms, zamindari abolition, declining importance of land revenue and public credit system began to alter rural areas.
- The period after 1947 was characterised by two major social movements.
- The Naxalite struggle and the 'new farmer's movements.' The Naxalite movement started from the region of Naxalbari (1967) in Bengal.

New social Movements among Peasants

- The so called 'new farmer's movements began in the 1970s in Punjab and Tamil Nadu.
- These movements were regionally oganised, were non-party, and involved farmers rather than peasants (farmers are said to be market-involved as both commodity producers and purchasers).
- The basic ideology of the movement was strongly anti-state and anti-urban.
- The focus of demands were 'price and related issues' (for example price procurement, remunerative prices, prices for agricultural inputs, taxation, non-repayment of loans).
- Novel methods of agitation were used: blocking of roads and railways, refusing politicians' and bureaucrats' entry to villages, and so on.

- It has been argued that the farmers' movements have broadened their agenda and ideology and include environment and women's issues.
- Therefore, they can be seen as a part of the worldwide 'new social movements'.

Workers' Movements

- Factory production began in India in the early part of the 1860s.
- The general pattern of trade set up by the colonial regime was one under which raw materials were procured from India and goods manufactured in the United Kingdom were marketed in the colony.
- These factories were, thus established in the port towns of Calcutta (Kolkata) and Bombay (Mumbai).
- Later factories were also set up in Madras (Chennai). Tea plantations in Assam were established as early as in 1839.
- In the early stages of colonialism, labour was very cheap as the colonial government did not regulate either wages or working conditions.
- The trade unions emerged later, workers did protest. Their actions then were, however, more spontaneous than sustained.
- In September and October 1917 there were around 30 recorded strikes. Jute workers in Calcutta struck work.
- In Madras, the workers of Buchingham and Carnatic Mills (Binny's) struck work for increased wages. Textile workers in Ahmedabad struck work for increase in wages by 50 per cent (Bhowmick 2004).

Formation of Trade Unions

- The first trade union was established in April 1918 in Madras by B.P. Wadia, a social worker and member of the Theosophical Society.
- During the same year, Mahatma Gandhi founded the Textile Labour Association (TLA).
- In 1920 the All India Trade Union Congress (AITUC) was formed in Bombay.
- The AITUC was a broad-based organisation involving diverse ideologies.
- The main ideological groups were the communists led by S.A. Dange and M.N. Roy, the moderates led by M. Joshi and V.V. Giri and the nationalist movements which involved people like Lala Lajpat Rai and Jawaharlal Nehru.
- The formation of the AITUC made the colonial government more cautious in dealing with labour.
- It attempted to grant workers some concessions in order to contain unrest. In 1922 the government passed the fourth Factories Act which reduced the working day to 10 hours.

- And in 1926, the Trade Unions Act was passed, which provided for registration of trade unions and proposed some regulations.
- By the mid-1920s, the AITUC had nearly 200 unions affiliated to it and its membership stood at around 250,000.
- During the last few years of British rule the communists gained considerable control over the AITUC.
- The Indian National Congress chose to form another union called the Indian National Trade Union Congress (INTUC) in May 1947.
- The split in the AITUC in 1947 paved the way for further splits on the line of political parties.

Caste Based Movements

The Dalit Movement

- The word Dalit is commonly used in Marathi, Hindi, Gujarati and many other Indian languages, meaning the poor and oppressed persons.
- It was first used in the new context in Marathi by neo-Buddhist activists, the followers of Babasaheb Ambedkar in the early 1970s.
- It refers to those who have been broken, ground down by those above them in a deliberate way.
- There has not been a single, unified Dalit movement in the country now or in the past.
- Notwithstanding differences in the nature of Dalit movements and the meaning of identity, there has been a common quest for equality, self-dignity and eradication of untouchability.
- This can be seen in the Satnami Movement of the Chamars in the Chattisgarh plains in eastern MP, Adi Dharma Movement in Punjab, the Mahar Movement in Maharashtra, the socio-political mobilisation among the Jatavas of Agra and the Anti-Brahman Movement in south India.
- Dalit literature is squarely opposed to the Chaturvarna system and caste hierarchy which it considers as responsible for crushing the creativity and very existence of lower castes.

Backward Class Castes Movements

- The term 'Backward Classes' has been in use in different parts of the country since the late 19th Century.
- It began to be used more widely in Madras presidency since 1872, in the princely state of Mysore since 1918, and in Bombay presidency since 1925.
- From the 1920s, a number of organisations united around the issue of caste sprang up in different parts of the country.

- These included the United Provinces Hindu Backward Classes League, All-India Backward Classes Federation, All India Backward Classes League.
- In 1954, 88 organisations were counted working for the Backward Classes.

The Tribal Movements

- Many of the tribal movements have been largely located in the so called 'tribal belt' in middle India, such as the Santhals, Hos, Oraons, Mundas in Chota Nagpur and the Santhal Parganas.

Jharkhand

- Jharkhand is one of the newly formed states of India, carved out of south Bihar in the year 2000.
- The social movement for Jharkhand had a charismatic leader in Birsa Munda, an adivasi who led a major uprising against the British. After his death, Birsa became an important icon of the movement.
- Stories and songs about him can be found all over Jharkhand.
- The memory of Birsa's struggle was also kept alive by writing.
- Christian missionaries working in south Bihar were responsible for spreading literacy in the area. Literate adivasis began to research and write about their history and myths.
- Literate adivasis were also in a position to get government jobs so that, over time, a middle-class adivasi intellectual leadership emerged that formulated the demand for a separate state and lobbied for it in India and abroad.
- Within south Bihar, adivasis shared a common hatred of dikus - migrant traders and moneylenders who had settled in the area and grabbed its wealth, impoverishing the original residents.
- The issues against which the leaders of the movement in Jharkand agitated were:
- acquisition of land for large irrigation projects and firing ranges;
- survey and settlement operations, which were held up, camps closed down, etc.
- collection of loans, rent and cooperative dues, which were resisted;
- nationalisation of forest produce which they boycotted

The North East

- The process of state formation initiated by the Indian government following the attainment of independence generated disquieting trends in all the major hill districts in the region.

- Conscious of their distinct identity and traditional autonomy the tribes were unsure of being incorporated within the administrative machinery of Assam.
- One of the key issues that bind tribal movements from different parts of the country is the alienation of tribals from forest lands.
- In this sense ecological issues are central to tribal movement

The Women's Movement

The 19th Century Social Reform Movements And Early Women's Organisation

- The Women's India Association (WIA) (1917), All India Women's Conference (AIWC) (1926) and National Council for Women in India (NCWI) (1925) are ready names of organisations that we can mention.
- For instance, the AIWC began with the idea that 'women's welfare' and 'politics' were mutually exclusive.
- Agrarian Struggles And Revolts: Women participated along with men in struggles and revolts originating in tribal and rural areas in the colonial period. The Tebhaga movement in Bengal, the Telangana arms struggle from the erstwhile Nizam's rule, and the Warli tribal's revolt against bondage in Maharashtra are some examples.

- Post-1947: In the mid-1970s, there was a renewal of the women's movement in India. Some call it the second phase of the Indian women's movement. There was the growth of what is termed as the autonomous women's movements. The term 'autonomy' referred to the fact that they were 'autonomous' or independent from political parties as distinct from those women's organisations that had links with political parties.
- Gender identities: There has also been greater recognition that both men and women are constrained by the dominant gender identities.
- For instance, men in patriarchal societies feel they must be strong and successful. It is not, manly, to express oneself emotionally.
- A gender-just society would allow both men and women to be free.
- This of course rests on the idea that for true freedom to grow and develop, injustices of all kind have to end.
- The idea of gender-just society is based upon two important factors - educated women with multiple roles and improved sex ratio.
- The programme of the Government of India, Beti Bachao, Beti Padhao Yojana is an important effort in the actualisation of a gender-just society.

Exercise

1. **Assertion (A):** A social movement requires sustained collective action over time.

   Reason (R): Spontaneous, disorganised protest cannot be called a social movement either.

   (a) Both A and R is true and R is the correct explanation of A

   (b) Both A and R is true and R is not the correct explanation of A

   (c) A is true and R is false

   (d) A is false and R is true

2. To change the existing social and political arrangements through gradual, incremental steps, is the following type of social movement -

   (a) Redemptive

   (b) Revivalist

   (c) Reformist

   (d) Revolutionary

3. The Bolshevik revolution in Russia that deposed the Tsar to create a communist state and the Naxalite movement in India that seeks to remove oppressive landlords and state officials, is the following type of social movement-

   (a) Redemptive

   (b) Revivalist

   (c) Reformist

   (d) Revolutionary

4. What was the reason behind Chipko Movement?

   (a) To save the oak and rhododendron forests near the villages.

   (b) To save ecology from road construction in ecological fragile area.

   (c) To save environment from deforestation for industrial purpose.

   (d) None of the above

5. Which of the following government's initiative seeks to create a balance, structure and quality in India's ecology?
- (a) Namami Gange
- (b) Swachchh Bharat Abhiyan
- (c) Both (a) and (b)
- (d) PM Urja Ganga Yojana

6. Which of the following statements are correct about Bardoli Satyagraha?
- I. It was a no tax campaign.
- II. It was part of nationwide non-cooperation movement.
- III. Farmers refused to pay land revenue to the British revenue collector.
- (a) I and II   (b) II and III
- (c) I and III   (d) All of the above

7. Which of the following was the first peasant organization?
- (a) All India Kisan Sabha
- (b) Bihar Provincial Kisan Sabha
- (c) UP Provincial Kisan Sabha
- (d) All India Peasant Organization

8. Choose the incorrect statement:
- (a) Peasant organizations demanded freedom from economic exploitation.
- (b) Telangana Movement was a struggle of sharecroppers in Bengal.
- (c) Tebhaga Movement was supported by Kisan Sabha and the Communist Party of India (CPI).
- (d) In 1920, protests against British government took place due to their forest policies.

9. Which of the following movement directed against the feudal conditions in the princely state of Hyderabad and was led by the CPI?
- (a) Deccan riots
- (b) Tebhaga Movement
- (c) Telangana Movement
- (d) Champaran Satyagrah

10. Which of the following are features of New Farmer's Movement after independence?
- I. These were regionally oganised, non-party and involved farmers rather than peasants.
- II. The basic ideology of the movement was strongly anti-state and anti-urban.
- III. The focus of demands were 'price and related issues'.
- (a) I and II   (b) II and III
- (c) I and III   (d) All of the above

11. Which of the following personality organized the first trade union?
- (a) B P Wadia   (b) S N Dange
- (c) M N Roy   (d) V V Giri

12. "A struggle to be touched" was a struggle known as -
- (a) Anti- Untouchability movement
- (b) Dalit movement
- (c) Land revenue agitation
- (d) Farmer's agitation

13. Which of the following are Dalit movements?
- I. Satnami movement
- II. Adi Dharma movement
- III. Jatavas movement
- (a) I only
- (b) II and III
- (c) I and II
- (d) All of the above

14. Spread of literacy in South Bihar was seen due to following reason?
- (a) Due to introduction of western education
- (b) Christian missionary
- (c) Introduction of civil services
- (d) All of the above

15. Which of the following were the issues of agitation in Jharkhand?
- I. Acquisition of land for large irrigation projects and firing ranges
- II. Survey and settlement operations
- III. Collection of loans, rent and cooperative dues
- IV. Nationalisation of forest produce
- (a) I, II and III
- (b) II, III and IV
- (c) III and IV
- (d) All of the above

16. Arrange the following women's organization in the correct chronological order:
- I. All India Women's Conference
- II. National Council for Women in India
- III. Women's India Association
- (a) III - II - I   (b) I - II - III
- (c) II - I - III   (d) I - III - II

17. The key issue which bind tribal movements from different parts of the country was -
- (a) Lack of education and modernization
- (b) Discrimination on the basis of race
- (c) Alienation of tribals from forest lands.
- (d) Atrocities of land lords for the land revenue

18. Which of the following statements are correct regarding All India Trade Union Council?

 I. It was formed in Bombay where diverse ideologies of communist, nationalists and liberals came together.

 II. It attempted to grant workers some concessions in order to contain unrest.

 III. V. V. Giri, Lala Lajpath Rai and Jawaharlal Nehru represented nationalist ideology in this.

 (a) I and II (b) II and III

 (c) III only (d) All of the above

19. Textile Labor Association was formed by the following leader?

 (a) S A Dange (b) Mahatma Gandhi

 (c) Lala Lajpat Rai (d) M N Roy

20. Choose the incorrect statement:

 (a) The creation of welfare states in the capitalist nations of Western Europe was partly due to political pressure by capitalists.

 (b) Movements in Soviet Union, China, and Cuba, led to the reform of capitalism.

 (c) Capitalism and colonialism have usually been interlinked through forms of imperialism.

 (d) Nationalist movements have mobilised against rule by a foreign power as well as against the dominance of foreign capital.

Answer Keys

1. (b)	2. (c)	3. (d)	4. (a)	5. (c)	6. (a)	7. (b)	8. (b)	9. (c)	10. (d)
11. (a)	12. (b)	13. (d)	14. (b)	15. (d)	16. (a)	17. (c)	18. (a)	19. (b)	20. (a)

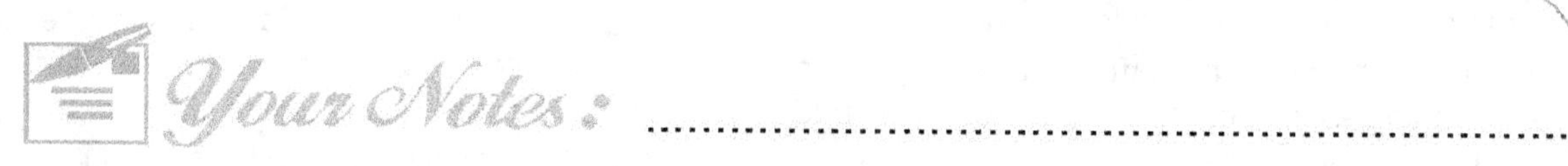 *Your Notes :* ....